Janus Secundus

MEDIEVAL & RENAISSANCE

TEXTS & STUDIES

VOLUME 143

RENAISSANCE MASTERS 2

Richard J. Schoeck
General Editor

Janus Secundus

by
DAVID PRICE

MEDIEVAL & RENAISSANCE TEXTS & STUDIES
Tempe, Arizona
1996

Library of Congress Cataloging-in-Publication Data

Price, David, 1957–
    Janus Secundus / by David Price.
        p. cm. — (Renaissance Masters ; v. 2) (Medieval & Renaissance texts
& studies ; v. 143)
    Includes bibliographical references.
    ISBN 0-86698-180-2
    1. Janus, Secundus, 1511–1536—Criticism and interpretation. 2. Love
poetry, Latin (Medieval and modern)—Netherlands—History and criticism.
3. Renaissance—Netherlands. 4. Humanists—Netherlands. I. Title.
PA8580.Z5P75 1995
871'.04—dc20   95-2655
                                               CIP

∞
This book was edited and produced
by MRTS at SUNY Binghamton.
This book is made to last.
It is set in Garamond Antiqua typeface,
smyth-sewn, and printed on acid-free paper
to library specifications.

Printed in the United States of America

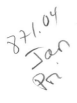

Fig. 1. Jan Gossaert van Mabuse's portrait of an unknown subject, probably the poet Janus Secundus. The cartouche reads "tu michi causa doloris." Reproduced courtesy of Staatliche Kunstsammlungen Kassel.

To George Schoolfield

Contents

List of Illustrations

Acknowledgments

Renaissance poetry in vernacular languages still holds great interest for scholars and general readers, as it always will. Latin Renaissance poetry, the subject of this book, no longer attracts a general readership for the simple reason that nowadays Latin poses a difficult impediment to most readers, even to many of the best educated. Latin poetry, now, almost always requires some form of mediation.

No one, however, seriously questions the historical importance or the intrinsic value of much Latin poetry. And it would be an error to assume the posture, as frequently happens in studies of Latin Renaissance poetry, that this research presents a neglected author to a forgetful world. Janus Secundus has never been entirely forgotten. His historical importance, especially his impact on Ronsard and the *Pléiade* as well as on German and English poetry of the seventeenth century, has always been acknowledged. My goal, rather, is to present new perspectives on his poetry and to do so in the context of a brief but comprehensive study, encompassing both Secundus's entire oeuvre and the important insights of earlier critics. And, if my optimism may be excused, this book is intended for the specialist and also for those generally interested in Renaissance poetry and the history of the classical tradition. In order to make my discussions as well as the poetry itself more accessible, I have provided relatively literal translations of all the Latin.

Anyone who pursues interests in Renaissance Latin poetry and who finds collegial and material support, as I have been most fortunate to do, ought to be deeply grateful. And I am. My greatest debt remains to George Schoolfield. It is not just that he has shared his erudition and many insights with me and, for that matter, all his students and colleagues. He has also done so in stimulating and uniquely entertaining ways. As far as the present study is concerned, I should add that his book on Secundus, which quite accidentally was among the first books on Renaissance poetry I read in graduate school, has served as a basis for my elaborations.

I am also grateful to Valerie Hotchkiss and Hubert Heinen for reading and discussing a draft of this book with me. Each of them corrected several blunders and pointed out infelicities. More importantly, conversations with them about poetry have kept me going, as it were, over the past few years and have certainly influenced my outlook.

This book would not exist were it not for the interest of Richard Schoeck and Mario DiCesare, two scholars who, in addition to pursuing their own research, have expended considerable energy for many years to support the work of others. I am grateful to Professor Schoeck for encouraging this work and to Professor DiCesare for accepting it for publication at MRTS. I also wish to acknowledge the helpful remarks of two anonymous readers as well as the patient and expert assistance of the staff at MRTS, especially Valerie Adamcyk, Assistant Editor, and Lori Vandermark, Production Manager.

Research, especially study at distant libraries, was made considerably easier with the support of the German Academic Exchange Service during the summer of 1991. I also worked on this as well as a broader study of Renaissance poetry with the assistance of a Beinecke Fellowship in May 1993. The staff at the Beinecke Library was enormously pleasant and helpful. I am also grateful to Fred Robinson for his kind attention during my stay at Yale and in particular for his critique of several essays I had written.

Portions of chapter four appeared as "The Poetics of License in Janus Secundus's *Basia*," in *Sixteenth Century Journal* 23 (1992): 289–301; I am grateful for permission to use that material here.

1 An Introduction

Parva seges satis est, satis est requiescere lecto
si licet et solito membra levare toro.
    Tibullus 1.1

[The harvest of a small field is enough; it is enough if I may sleep
on my bed and rest my limbs on my familiar mattress.]

Janus Secundus (1511–1536) has long been recognized as one of the
most significant and enduring poets of the Renaissance. Though also
a master of the ode and epigram as well as a prolific writer of funeral
poetry and poetic epistles, he has come down to us as *the* outstanding
Latin love poet of the northern Renaissance.

Some have claimed, with predictable hyperbole, that he surpassed
those ancient poets, such as Catullus, Tibullus, Propertius, and Ovid,
whom he imitated.[1] However that may be, there is no doubt that he
is one of the few Renaissance Latin poets whose works can be appre-
ciated on equal footing with his Roman forebears.[2] While his reputation has never rivalled that of his models, Secundus's poetry has seldom wanted for receptive readers. His renown grew during his brief
lifetime—he lived but twenty-four years—became immense during the
sixteenth and seventeenth centuries and has continued, as indicated
by a steady stream of editions, translations, imitations, and studies,
until this very day. Most conspicuous among his readers have been
other poets: Ronsard, Labé, Opitz, Fleming, Huygens, Milton, and

---

[1] Janus Dousa, for example, made the obvious pun, saying that he was second to no ancient writers: "ceterum nulli antiquorum meo iudicio secundus."
Quoted from Secundus, *Opera omnia*, ed. Burmannus and Bosscha, 2:289. Here-
after cited as BB.

[2] This has been the opinion of virtually all who have read Secundus. See BB,
1: xxxv (for the opinion of Burmann) and BB, 2:289 (for Scriverius's tribute).

Goethe—to name but a few examples from several national litera-tures—number among his admirers.[1] They and others have acknowl-edged their debt to him either directly in encomiastic verses, or indi-rectly in poetic imitations. No less a literary authority than Johann Gottfried Herder claimed, humorously but tellingly, that Goethe was but "the third Johann" of amatory poetry, the first having been John the Evangelist (John 15:12: "That you love one another as I have loved you") and the second having been, of course, Janus Secundus.[2] Secundus left behind a remarkably diverse oeuvre. After the poet's death, Théodore de Bèze (1519–1605), who would make his mark as successor to Calvin at Geneva, was one of the first to admire his versatility:

> Excelsum seu condit Epos, magnique Maronis
> Luminibus officere studet:
> Sive leves Elegos alternaque carmina, raptus
> Nasonis impetu, canit:
> Sive lyram variis sic aptat cantibus, ut se
> Victum erubescat Pindarus:
> Sive iocos, blandosque sales Epigrammate miscet,
> Clara invidente Bilbili:
> Unus quatuor haec sic praestitit ille Secundus,
> Secundus ut sit nemini.[3]

[Whether he composes lofty epic, desiring to lessen the bril-liance of great Vergil, or, carried off by the force of Ovid, he sings light elegies and songs in distich, or whether he tunes the lyre so well for diverse odes that Pindar is ashamed to have been bested, or mixes jests and charming witticism epigrammati-cally—while Martial envies their fame—that Secundus, though one poet, so excelled in these four genres as to be second to no one.]

---

[1] A list of his imitators would be lengthy. For discussions of Secundus's in-fluence, see the following: Van Tieghem, *La littérature latine de la Renaissance*, 74–78; Crane, *Johannes Secundus*, 42–79; Secundus, *Basia*, ed. Ellinger, x–xlv; and Endres, *Joannes Secundus*, 31–35.

[2] See Crane, *Johannes Secundus*, 76–77.

[3] Quoted from BB, 2:284.

Secundus might have disagreed with Bèze's praise of epic since, despite late plans for the *Bellum Tunetanum*, he was opposed to writing epic. (Bèze, obviously thinking metrically, must be referring to Secundus's poems in hexameter, such as his Vergilian eclogue[1] and some of the poetic epistles.) The emphasis on the small forms—elegy, ode, and epigram—indicates the preference of Secundus's voice for the short poem, but also its rich variety and the astonishing mastery of complex Roman metrics. In a portrait by Jan van Scorel (which survives only in copies), a slender volume lies before Secundus on which is written that his life's work comprises but ten books.[2] (See fig. 2.) These books, which were assembled by Secundus's brothers, still constitute the core of his oeuvre: three books of elegies; one book of *Basia* (Kisses); one book of epigrams;[3] one book of odes; two books of poetic letters; one book of funeral poetry; and one book of *Sylvae* (i.e., miscellaneous poetry in different meters). In addition to a few poetic fragments and a few prose letters, there are two prose itineraries.[4] That, along with twelve sculpted medallions, is what survives from the hand of Janus Secundus.

Secundus's aesthetic evokes an Alexandrian ideal of poetry. Valorization of the small lyric and elegiac forms over the epic recalls the Callimachean "Big book, big evil," though any Alexandrian orientation was certainly derived indirectly through Catullus and the Roman eroticists. In particular, Secundus's works embody the Catullan ideal of nugatory poetics, as expressed by Catullus in *Carmina* 1 where he calls his poetry "nugae" (trifles). Indeed, it is not at all accidental that one of Secundus's dedicatory poems is based on Catullus 1:

---

[1] For an edition and English translation of Secundus's eclogue (*Sylvae* 5), see Martyn, "Ioannes Secundus: Orpheus and Eurydice."

[2] The copy obviously dates from after the 1541 edition of Secundus's works. The original, done during Secundus's lifetime, could not have depicted a book with the title of "Carmin. Io. Secund. lib. X."

[3] There are, actually, two books of epigrams in the edition of 1541, though the second book is so slight and of such marginal importance—it consists of but seventeen translations of epigrams from the *Greek Anthology*—that it may not have been counted as a separate book of poetry. These poems are introduced (without the designation "liber") with the modest phrase "Epigrammata quaedam e Graeco versa" (fol. K5ʳ). The edition of 1541 is cited according to *Opera: nunc primum in lucem edita* (1541; repr. Nieuwkoop: de Graaf, 1969).

[4] Dekker, *Janus Secundus*, 49, has argued convincingly that the second of the *Itineraries*, printed by Daniel Heinsius (1618) and Burmann-Bosscha as Secundus's work, was almost certainly written by Hadrianus Marius.

Cui mitto calidos novos amores,
Nec satis lepidos, nec expolitos?
Nimirum tibi: namque tu putabis
Meas esse aliquid, Rumolde, nugas,
Adsuetus genium probare nostrum,
Iam tum, quum imperio tuo sonabam
Parvus carmina renuente lingua.
Ergo habe tibi quidquid hoc amorum est:
Et quidquid venit a meis Camenis,
Totum crede tui laboris esse.

(*Epigrams* 1.49.1–10)

[To whom do I send my new, hot loves, though they are neither charming nor polished enough? To you, of course. For
you, Rumoldus, used to consider my trifles to be something and
you used to endorse my talent—even when, under your tutelage,
I, as a boy, used to sound out songs with an uncooperative tongue.
Therefore, accept whatever these love poems have and know that
whatever comes from my muses is entirely your work.]

The nugatory aesthetic deprecates its subject matter, with conscious irony, as being trivial, but trivial in the specific sense that it
has little consequence for public affairs. For example, several of Secundus's poems reject the epic (*Elegies* 1.1; *Epigrams* 1.58; and *Poetic
Epistles* 2.6), recalling the ancient genre of the *recusatio* (refusal).[1]
When Secundus expresses aversion for the august style of epic, he
also refuses to write of the world of politics and great men. This posture, which I will discuss below in more detail, not only eschews the
idea of poetry operating in service to God or state (or rulers), but
also defends poetic liberty from the encroachment of those forces.
The small world of the poet, his loves, friends and experiences are
proper literary subjects that stand, implicitly, in a binary opposition
to the "big world" of public affairs, social morality, Christianity, etc.
Furthermore, where this aesthetic disappoints political expectations
or is at variance with a socioliterary code, the poet can take recourse
to the ancient poets, such as Catullus, Ovid, or Martial, for legitimacy, if not respectability.

---

[1] See Endres and Gold, "Joannes Secundus and his Roman Models," 282–86,
for a discussion of *Elegies* 1.1.

Secundus does not, however, consistently take this posture, since
he, as we will see, was willing to compose political and even panegyric poetry. Nonetheless, his political poetry is also in the condensed
small forms, and he tends to describe political figures in a light tone,
occasionally with hints of irony. The love poet writing elegies and
odes on political topics, of course, has classical antecedents. One
thinks of Catullus's lampoons of Caesar, Tibullus's service to Mes-
sala, not to mention Ovid's (necessary) bows to Augustus or the pa-
tronage enjoyed—and laudatory poems delivered—by Horace and
Propertius.

A northern humanist and, moreover, a humanist poet of a later
generation, Secundus did not create a new poetics through unmediat-
ed study of ancient poets. Of course, direct access to ancient poetry
nurtured his writing—he certainly committed large amounts of Roman poetry to memory. Nonetheless, the inspiration and in large part
the authority for writing erotic poetry comes from Italian humanists,
even though, clearly, they were not studied or emulated with the
same intensity accorded the ancient poets.

As is the case with the German love poet Conrad Celtis (1459–
1508), northern humanists often betray an inferiority complex vis-à-
vis the Italian poets. Secundus, however, speaks with an unusually
confident voice, as best indicated perhaps by the infrequency in his
oeuvre of gratuitously displaying recondite knowledge of classical
culture—a trait that often spoils humanist poetry. His eye, though,
was trained on the Italians. In an elegy to Erasmus (*Elegies* 3.5), for
example, he felt obliged to praise the Netherlands as a seat of high
culture and to eulogize his country as the equal of Italy—it had, after
all, produced the unequaled Erasmus:

> ... Felix quae talem terra tulisti!
> Tu mihi vel magno non minor es Latio.
>
> (lines 23–24)

[Netherlands, you are blessed to have born such a man. You
are, I think, equal even to great Latium.]

Secundus himself left a record of the Italian poets who were highest on his reading list. In a literary elegy to the now obscure Italian
poet Girolamo Montio (*Elegies* 3.7), he narrates a dream in which the
goddess Elegy appeared to him in the costume of Latium to describe
the Italian humanists who, along with the ancient poets, created her

form.[1] Secundus mentions Tito Vespasiano Strozzi (1424–1505),[2] his son Ercole (ca. 1473–1508), Pietro Bembo (1470–1547), Marco Girolamo Vida (ca. 1485–1566) and, then, the four Italian poets he admired most: Giovanni Pontano (1426–1503), Jacopo Sannazaro (1456–1530),[3] Michele Marullo (ca. 1453–1500), and Andrea Alciati (1492–1550). For Secundus, Alciati was, more than anything else, the model of the poet-lawyer, though his interest in the epigram and the eroticism of the *Greek Anthology* left their mark, too. There are several reminiscences of Sannazaro and Pontano, perhaps the greatest Latin love poets from Italy, in Secundus's poetry. Pontano's elegance and humor in the epigram and elegy and the distinctive lightness and inventiveness of his *epicedia* make him perhaps the poet from Italy most like Secundus.[4] Nonetheless, Marullo's sharp wit and passion, not to mention his brashness, made a deep impression. Secundus composed two epigrams that record his initial reading of Marullo and immediately acknowledge an indebtedness. In *Epigrams* 1.32, he returns a volume of Marullo to its owner, he says, without loss of a single verse, though an enormous treasury of poetry has been extracted. In *Epigrams* 1.33, he connects Marullo's aesthetic to that of ancient elegists, apostrophizing him as the reincarnation of Tibullus. Marullo was something of a controversial writer, as his poetry, especially his hymns, seemed to many to be offensively pagan; Christianity was certainly not a prominent force in his works, nor was it to play a significant role for Secundus. In the *Dialogus Ciceronianus*, for example, Erasmus wishes that Marullo had had "minus ... paganitatis"[5] (less paganism). It is also, perhaps, a tribute to Marullo that Secundus named the lover of the *Basia* Neaera, as that was the name of Marullo's beloved. Above all, the appreciation of Marullo's nugatory poetics suggests a quality found in Secundus: "[L]epidos cum gravitate iocos" (witty and charming poems which have dignity; *Epigrams* 1.33.2), though said of Marullo's poetry, describes the Secun-

---

[1] With the personification of "Elegy," Secundus recalls Ovid, *Amores* 3.1.

[2] Strozzi was well-known as an imitator of Tibullus and as the author of six books of *Erotica*.

[3] Sannazaro's Latin name, which Secundus naturally uses, was Actius Syncerus.

[4] Guépin, *De Kunst van Janus Secundus*, prints several poems by Pontano related to the *Basia*.

[5] Erasmus, *Dialogus Ciceronianus*, ed. Mesnard, in *Opera omnia*, 1.2:666.

dian art of combining levity and irony with expressions of serious-
ness and torment.

Scholarship on Secundus has, in the main, addressed biographical
and philological issues—and the achievements in these areas have
been significant.[1] Recently, Alfred Dekker, whose book is the most
extensive biography and, moreover, lays a new foundation for philological investigation, stated not only that much more philological
study is needed, but also that the time is unripe for interpretative
studies. This opinion has some validity but is, overall, untenable. In
the aftermath of the discovery of the Bodleian manuscript, which Secundus's brothers Hadrianus Marius and Nicolaus Grudius prepared
for the printer of the first collected edition (which appeared in 1541[2]),
a new critical edition is absolutely necessary; yet one cannot con-
strain scholars and readers from study of such an important poet for
an indefinite period. The manuscript proves that the brothers altered
poems for their edition, though restorations of what was probably
Secundus's text really do not produce a substantially new poet, different from the one we have come to know through the editions of
the brothers, Scriverius, or Burmann and Bosscha. As a new critical
edition is not likely to appear for several years, I have quoted Secundus from the Burmann-Bosscha edition and checked those citations
against a microfilm copy of the Bodleian manuscript for significant
variation, each instance of which has been noted.[3] (See fig. 3.)

In addition to biographical and textual issues, scholarship has ex-
plored the poet's relationship to his sources. Though accorded much
effort, identification of antecedents still warrants more attention, as
many reminiscences of classical and Renaissance authors have not
been noted by Burmann-Bosscha and others. On a more theoretical
level, scholars have analyzed Secundus's approach to imitation, a per-
ennial issue in the study of Renaissance poets.

Though influence is undeniably a crucial topic, most scholars
have been preoccupied with the interplay of convention and individuality, or, as Spitzer put it, "how to give the flavor of *new* personal

---

[1] Dekker's biographical sketch, *Janus Secundus*, 19–96, is authoritative.

[2] The most thorough description of the Bodleian manuscript is Tuynman,
"De Handschriften en overige bronnen vor de teksten van Secundus."

[3] For the several poems published during Secundus's lifetime, I was able to
consult Dekker's thorough textual descriptions.

emotions to the *traditional* Latin vocabulary."[1] This question informs Nichols's well-founded view of Secundus as a poet who combined "experience and literary tradition ... to form a seamless garment."[2] Obviously, there is no theoretical flaw in approaching Renaissance poetry from the perspective of influence. In practice, however, this approach has fostered a tendency to exclude other kinds of analysis, especially the question of how political concepts of literature could inform Renaissance lyric.

George Schoolfield's is the most comprehensive study of the poetry. In particular, he, too, appreciates the affinities and discontinuities between Secundus and his models, and he identifies, for the first time, the distinctive element of Secundus's erotic poetry, namely, its vivid and explicit representations of desire: "The intense perceptions and representation of physical love by Janus have kept the *Basia* alive, and not, when all is said and done, his ingenuity, elegance, or even coinage of phrases, however important these qualities may have been for his literary survival."[3] J. P. Guépin has continued the biographical-philological tradition of Secundian scholarship, offering, above all, a diverse commentary on the *Basia* and a few other poems. His principal achievement is the presentation of the Italian Renaissance eroticists who, as had already been known, inspired Secundus.[4]

The two traditional approaches to Secundus—philological-biographical study and analysis of influence—though sound, require an enlargement or extension of purview. Above all, the biographical paradigm needs inversion: instead of using the poems as a source for constructing a Secundus biography, it is necessary to define how the self-stylizing autobiography implicit in his works, whether reliable or wholly fictionalized, functions as a central trope of amatory poetry. Autobiography informs the valorization of the poet's singular experi-

---

[1] Spitzer, "The Problem of Latin Renaissance Poetry," 942–43.

[2] Nichols, "The Renewal of Latin Poetry," 95.

[3] Schoolfield, *Janus Secundus*, 116.

[4] Guépin affixes, I feel, too much significance to Neoplatonism in his approach to the *Basia*. One cannot document any interest on the part of Secundus in Neoplatonism; rather, he has merely imitated a few poems from antiquity and the Renaissance which express Neoplatonic views. Indeed, one of the important accomplishments of Secundus is that he kept a non-philosophical (and non-allegorical) form of erotic poetry alive, which had a significant impact in the seventeenth century.

ences over social or political matters, and, by extension, the experience of art over the poetic recording of, say, political history. Those poems which reflect on art suggest an ideal of life as being constituted by experience as opposed to life defined by deeds or accomplishments. His imitative aesthetic accommodates experience—the alleged absence of which is a common red herring in scholarship on northern humanist poetry—by valorizing the experience of the imagination, or the specific experience of art, over other kinds of experience.

Moreover, imitation of the ancients is not just a stylistic device, but also a means of validating a concept of poetic freedom from political and moralistic constraints. Secundus seeks to offend audiences, sometimes by exemplifying a radical (obscene) level of poetic license, but he consistently grounds his transgressiveness in the imitation of Roman authors, creating, in a sense, the paradox of a conventional-transgressive poet. Instead of being a genuine record of actual "Erlebnis,"[1] love can be seen more appropriately, I shall argue, as a cipher for poetry, and the self-reflective apologies for his *métier* as an eroticist are, to a degree, general defenses of the ideal of poetic freedom. Similar to the thematic contrast between the larger world of society and politics and the subjective (constricted or insignificant) experience of the poet, is the rhetorical opposition Secundus sometimes creates between the audience and the poetic I, as most notably in the *Basia* (see chapter four) and in the *Epigrams* (see chapter five).

Transgression of sexual-social decorum, as in the naming, so to speak, of the lower body,[2] and resistance to ideologies of literature, as in the refusal to write commissioned political poetry, are important but not constant features of Secundus's poetry. His amatory aesthetic may resist a politically or moralistically defined concept of poetry, but he also composed explicitly political and encomiastic poetry (which will be discussed in chapter six). Furthermore, the brashness of his obscenity often is juxtaposed to the elegance of his high style. Indeed, the high and the low, the sublime and the pedestrian, are frequently coterminous in his poetry. I should also mention

---

[1] This is the approach of Ellinger, *Geschichte der neulateinischen Literatur*, 3/1: 28–75; see especially 74.

[2] For a useful discussion of the complexity of transgression, especially as it occurs in carnivalesque inversions, see Stallybrass and White, *The Politics and Poetics of Transgression*, especially 1–26.

that, in his defenses of the nugatory poetics and, more importantly, the low style, Secundus assumes a posture of being progressive. Nonetheless, his transgressive *modus scribendi* is also, perhaps unconsciously, complicit on occasions in misogynist ideology (as will be discussed in chapter four), which, though hardly unexpected in a Renaissance poet, qualifies the salutariness he attributes to license.

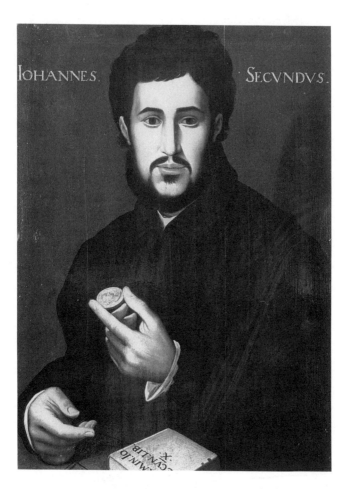

Fig. 2. Copy of Jan van Scorel's portrait of Janus Secundus
Reproduced courtesy of Haags Gemeentemuseum

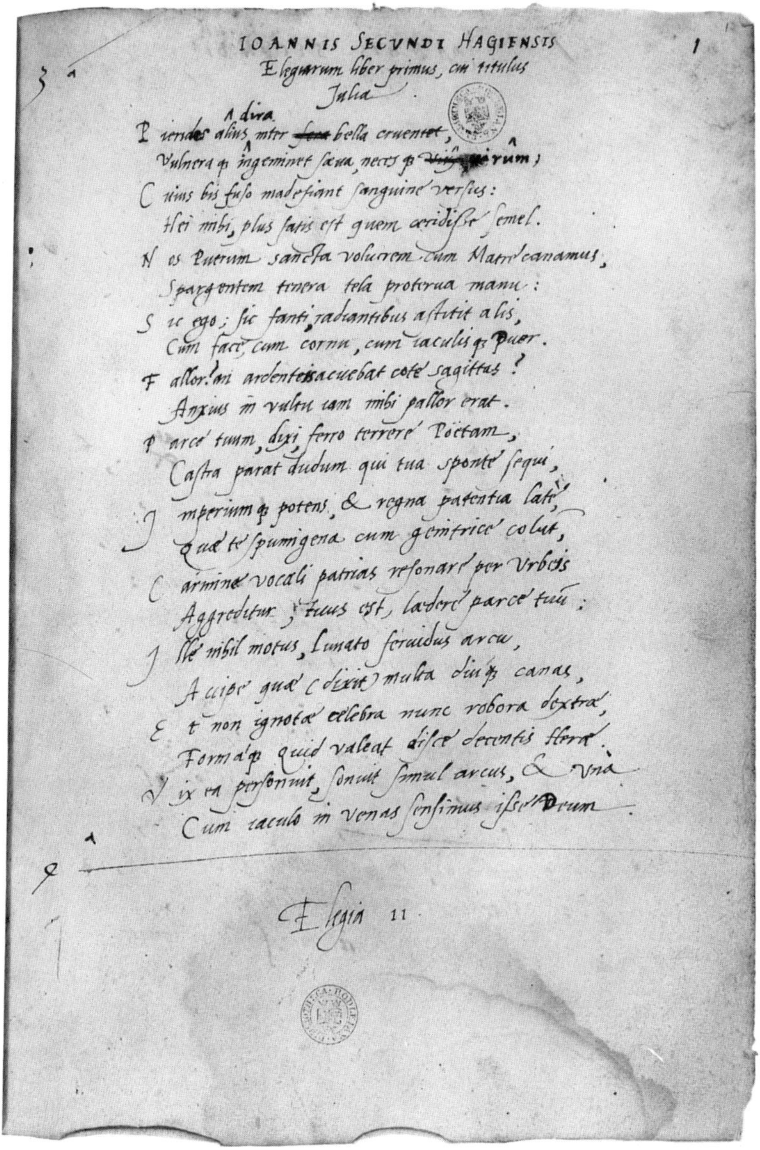

Fig. 3. A page from Bodleian MS. Rawl. G. 154
(The beginning of *Elegies* 1.1)
Reproduced courtesy of the Bodleian Library

2 The Life and Writings of Janus Secundus

Jan Second de qui la gloire
N'ira jamais defaillant.
Pierre de Ronsard, *Odes* 5.10

Few poets have been born to more auspicious circumstances than was Secundus. He was the youngest member of a family distinguished by its political and literary attainments. His father, Nicolaas Everaerts (1462–1532), held important governmental offices in the Netherlands and had also pursued literary and scholarly interests. Everaerts was educated at the University of Louvain, where, in 1493, he took the doctorate in both laws.[1] After a career as professor of law at Louvain, including the office of rector, he entered the highest ranks of the political-judicial bureaucracy of the Hapsburg Netherlands, when Philip the Handsome (1478–1506), son of Emperor Maximilian I (1459–1519), appointed him to the newly revived grand council of the Netherlands at Mechlin in 1505. He became president of the council of Holland in 1509, a tenure that lasted until 1528, when he was named president of the grand council of the Netherlands. He held this last office until his death in 1532.

According to all accounts,[2] Everaerts was a man of probity and learning: he carried out the duties of his offices effectively and without scandal; and, throughout his life, he kept apprised of the latest developments in the humanist world of letters. He is still remem-

---

[1] On Secundus's father, see Tracy, "Everaerts, Nicolaas," in *Contemporaries of Erasmus*, 1:446–47. There are slips, though, in Tracy's listing of letters from Erasmus to Everaerts. For a more thorough account, see ten Raa, "Everaerts, Nicolaas," *Nationaal Biografisch Woordenboek*, 7:214–31.

[2] See *Funeral Poems* 1, in BB, 2:97–109.

bered as the author of two important legal treatises[1] and, in particular, as one of Erasmus's correspondents. Although all the details of their relationship are not known, six letters by Erasmus to Everaerts survive as well as two others in which he is mentioned. In letter 1188, for example, Erasmus confesses a special faith in Everaerts's discretion,[2] and the letters in general document Erasmus's contact with the Everaerts family, though the degree of intimacy cannot be ascertained. (While there is no evidence that Secundus met Erasmus, it is entirely possible that Erasmus had been a guest at the Everaerts'; Secundus's epitaph for Erasmus, furthermore, has a rather detached tone, but we should remember that Secundus wrote it while seriously ill, shortly before his own death.[3]) Most of the letters indicate Erasmus's attempt to keep such an influential man as Everaerts abreast of his evolving views on the Reformation; they also suggest that Everaerts had a sympathetic ear for Erasmus's thoughts on ecclesiastical reform.[4]

Of the eighteen children born to Nicolaas Everaerts and Elisabeth van Bladel (1466/67–1547), nine are known to have lived into adulthood. One son, Petrus Hieronymus (ca. 1488–1529?),[5] entered the cloister, while the remaining five boys, including Secundus, pursued legal-political careers. With the exception of Franciscus († before 25 March 1534), about whom little is known,[6] Secundus kept in close contact with his brothers; he made several members of his family the subject of his poetry, principally by sending them literary epistles or by writing incidental poems for them. The prominence of his family in his poetry is paralleled by his many poetic tributes to friends,[7] the

---

[1] The legal treatises are *Topicorum seu de locis legalibus liber* and *Consilia sive responsa iuris*.

[2] Erasmus, *Opus epistolarum*, 4:446–48.

[3] *Funeral Poems* 22.

[4] In a letter dated 24 December 1525, Erasmus comments on Luther's marriage as a comic twist to the "Lutherana tragoedia," polemicizing, in the traditional fashion, against it as the liaison of a monk and a nun: "Duxit uxorem, monachus monacham" (Erasmus, *Opus epistolarum*, 6:240 [no. 1653]). The same letter also laments the bloodshed of the Peasants War, then raging in Germany.

[5] Secundus wrote an *epicedion* for him; see *Funeral Poems* 14.

[6] Franciscus became an imperial secretary to the grand council of the Netherlands. See Dekker, *Janus Secundus*, 65 (n. 16).

[7] Several of the poems in Book Three of the *Elegies* are addressed to friends, as is the majority of poems in the two books of *Poetic Epistles*.

result of which is that Secundus's poetry has a highly familiar tone. Nonetheless, familiarity is often the tonal setting for reflections on the experience of art since most of his acquaintances, it seems, had a significant connection to art or literature. Of the family members, Everardus Nicolai (1497/98–1561) was the recipient of the most poems (*Poetic Epistles* 1.1–4). Everardus followed closely in his father's footsteps, and, like him, crowned his career as president of the grand council of the Netherlands (1557–1561).[1]

Secundus and his two other brothers have entered the annals of literary history as the "tres fratres Belgae"[2] (the three brothers of the Low Countries). Nicolaus Grudius (1503/4–1570/71) and Hadrianus Marius (1509–1568) became distinguished poets in their own right and, unquestionably, nurtured the literary interests of their younger brother. Secundus addressed a few poems to them but, more importantly, seems to have sent them his poems on a regular basis for criticism.[3] The brothers ensured the survival and, in most cases, initial publication of Secundus's poetry. A few poems had appeared during his life and, shortly after his death, Michael Nerius published the *Basia* (Lugduni: Gryphius, 1539); Nicolaus Grudius and Hadrianus Marius, however, brought out the first collected edition of Secundus's poems in 1541.[4]

---

[1] For information on him, see ten Raa, "Nicolai, Everaert," *Nationaal Biografisch Woordenboek* 7:656–62.

[2] In the early seventeenth century, Bonaventura Vulcanius assembled and produced an anthology of poetry by the three brothers, *Poemata et effigies trium fratrum Belgarum* (1612).

[3] He addressed the encomiastic *Elegies* 2.1 to both Nicolaus Grudius and Hadrianus Marius, and also wrote a brief epithalamium for Grudius's second marriage (*Elegies* 2.10). Considerable energy and good humor inform their literary correspondences. Hadrianus, for example, once composed a parodistic reply to one of Secundus's more lugubrious poems from Spain, the "Patriae Desiderium" (*Elegies* 3.11). The parody is printed in *Delitiae c. poetarum Belgicorum*, ed. Gruterus, 3:426.

[4] There are a few problems with their edition. As indicated by the Bodleian MS. Rawl. G. 154, which was the printer's copy for the first edition, the printers introduced numerous alterations to the text, a few of which are not minor. They also suppressed several poems, especially those associated with Francis I and Henry VIII, so as to avoid political controversy. An interesting edition of Secundus, which printed his works along with those of Michele Marullo and the lesser artist Hieronymus Angerianus, was brought out by Ludovicus Martellus: *Poetae tres elegantissimi* (1582). Petrus Scriverius produced a somewhat more reliable text in 1619 and also restored the deleted poems. In 1631, Scriverius pub-

Nicolaus Grudius has been called a "curious amalgamation of the various talents which other members of the family represented separately."[1] He became secretary to the privy council of Charles V (1500–1558) and served in that capacity during Secundus's residence in Spain. Among other distinctions are his office as registrar of the Order of the Golden Fleece and his position as Philip II's general tax collector in the Brabant. However, at the order of Mary of Hungary (1505–1558), he was arrested 1 December 1553 on charges of embezzlement and held until October 1555.[2] The circumstances of his later life and death in Venice are somewhat mysterious, though it is clear that he died under a cloud of scandal. An important political figure until his arrest, he was yet more famous as a poet. Like Secundus, he composed love poetry, some of which was anthologized by Janus Gruterus (1560–1627) in the important collection *Delitiae c. poetarum Belgicorum* (1614).[3] In 1540 he published a book of political epigrams celebrating Charles V's entry into Valencia. Unlike his brothers, he also composed a sizable collection of religious poetry, most notably *Piorum poematum libri duo* (published in 1566).

Hadrianus Marius also had a successful career with a murky end, though of a different kind. For most of his adult life he served as chancellor of Gelderland and Zutphen (1547–1567). His last year was marred, however, by his appointment by the duke of Alba (1507–1582) to be one of the twelve judges sitting on a court which came to be known as the "Council of Blood" since it was to try (and hang) the iconoclasts of Brussels. Hadrianus, too, was an elegant latinist and sensitive poet, also anthologized by Gruterus. Of his love poetry, Secundus celebrated the "Cymba Amoris" (Boat of Love) in an endearingly hyperbolic passage:

> Ingeniose Mari! ventura in secula tecum

---

lished a second edition, based on a review of MS. Rawl. G. 154, with important improvements. Alfred M. M. Dekker plans a new critical edition. Until that appears, the standard edition remains the *Opera omnia* in two volumes edited by Petrus Bosscha and Petrus Burmann (1821). The edition of 1541 is available in reprint (1969).

[1] Schoolfield, *Janus Secundus*, 18.

[2] Van Leijenhorst, "Grudius, Nicolaus," in *Contemporaries of Erasmus*, 2:139–40.

[3] This anthology also contains a very large selection from Secundus's poetry; see *Delitiae c. poetarum Belgicorum*, ed. Gruterus, 4:146–352.

Me tua Cymba vehat, non grave pondus ero.
Cymba, renidentem qua mutet Cypria concham,
Quamque columbino praeferat ipsa iugo.
(*Elegies* 2.1.37–40)

[Ingenious Marius, may your "Boat" transport me with you
into the coming centuries; I shan't be heavy. The "Boat," for
which Venus would exchange her brilliant conch and which she
prefers to her dove-drawn chariot.]

With the exception of Elisabeth, little is known of Secundus's sisters. One sister, Catharina († 1540), is not mentioned in Secundus's oeuvre; another, Gulielma († after 1568), is only mentioned at the end of an exuberant letter sent to Everardus Nicolai when Secundus received his appointment as secretary to the archbishop of Toledo.[1] However, Elisabeth (ca. 1489–1558), celebrated in Latin as Isabella, appears to have had a share in the political and artistic talents of the family. She entered the convent of St. Agatha at Delft, where she distinguished herself as a painter and, moreover, eventually became abbess.[2] Furthermore, Secundus's testimony indicates that she was an accomplished latinist, though, as far as I can determine, none of her writings are now known:

> Salve, o feminei, soror, unica gloria sexus,
>   Inferior nullis Isaäbella viris.
> Gaudia quanta mihi, quantum iniecere stuporem,
>   Depicta articulis verba Latina tuis!
> Quam pia, quam lepida, et quam mellea, quamque
>   venusta!
>   Quam docta et cunctis illa polita modis!
> O quoties lecta illa mihi, quotiesque relecta,
>   Nec satiare oculos nec potuere animum.
> Macte animo, similem nullam cui nostra tulerunt,
>   Forte dabant olim secula prisca pares.
> Credo, aequare suum poterat quae carmine patrem,
>   Inclyta Nasonis filia talis erat.
> Tullia talis erat, docto dilecta parenti;

---

[1] See BB, 2:277, for the text of the letter.
[2] See ten Raa, "Nicolai, Elisabeth," *Nationaal Biografisch Woordenboek*, 7:652–56. Several of her miniatures survive.

Talis erat Gracchos quae tulit illa duos.
Sperare hac qualem licuisset ab arbore fructum,
Ni tam non apta consita staret humo!

(Poetic Epistles 1.5)

[Greetings, sister, singular glory of the female sex, Isabella, inferior to no man! What great pleasure, what amazement those Latin words, written by your hand, have given me. How pious, elegant, sweet and charming! How learned they were and polished in every way. How many times I read and reread them; still neither my eyes nor my soul ever wearied of them. Well done, my dear! Our age has brought no woman like you, though, by chance, the ancient age has provided some equals. I believe the famous daughter of Ovid, who could equal her father in poetry, was such a one; such a one was Tullia, beloved by her learned father; such a one was she who bore the two Gracchi.[1] One could have hoped for such fruit from this tree, were it not planted in such unsuitable soil!]

There were, of course, several other extremely learned women of the northern Renaissance, of whom Secundus would have heard. One thinks of Margaret More (1505–1544) who exerted a profound influence on Erasmus, and one could also mention Caritas Pirckheimer (1466–1532), whom the German poet Conrad Celtis praised so effusively in a letter composed in Sapphic strophes.[2] Secundus's praise of his sister's writing is instructive because it extols the qualities he sought in his own writing. The literary-critical terms used for the encomium are drawn from Catullus ("lepida ... venusta ... docta ... polita"),[3] all of which endorses a Catullan aesthetic of the short, witty poem, implying, furthermore, an interest in the erotic, though that is tempered somewhat by the prominence of "pia." Naturally, the poem also indicates that antiquity is the only meaningful touchstone for assessing Renaissance poetry. Nonetheless, in the compari-

---

[1] That is Cornelia, who was renowned for having declined to remarry in order to devote herself to the education of her children. The reference to her provides the transition to the idea of a literary woman nurturing a future male writer and stresses the condescension in Secundus's portrait of his sister as a female anomaly.

[2] See Rupprich, *Der Briefwechsel des Konrad Celtis*, 484–85.

[3] See, for example, the diction in Catullus's programmatic first poem.

son to antiquity, one cannot overlook the extreme condescension, despite the endorsement, toward a woman who would be a literary artist.

A great deal is known about Secundus's life, though, it seems, not quite enough to construct a reliable portrait of his character or personality. Rather, we know where he resided, with whom he had contact, and under what circumstances he wrote many of his poems. Despite the inability to draw a portrait of the man, Secundian scholarship is heavily biographical. That may be due to the simple fact that, in his poetry, Secundus often claims to be recording personal experiences.

Janus Secundus (or Joannes Nicolai Secundus Hagiensis) was born in The Hague on 15 November 1511.[1] He took the cognomen Secundus probably because his birth fell on the feast day of a certain martyr Secundinus, not, as has been thought, because he may have had an older brother named Janus who died as an infant. Perhaps after attending a primary school in The Hague, he took lessons, along with his brothers and a friend, Viglius van Aytta (Viglius Zuichemus, 1507–1577), from the renowned master Jacob Volkaerd (Jacobus Volcardus, † before March 1528). This instruction, which began, most likely, in 1520, continued until 1522, when Volcardus moved to Louvain. Thereupon, Rumoldus Stenemola (1491–1541) became his tutor in Latin and Greek. It is also likely that he then began studying law at home, probably under his father's direction. While Volcardus was the first to develop Secundus's muse,[2] it was Stenemola who sustained and fostered the literary development of the Everaerts boys. And Secundus was genuinely appreciative, it seems, since in later years he sent his former master a bundle of poetry with a dedication parodying Catullus's "Cui dono lepidum novum libellum?"[3] (To whom do I dedicate this charming, new, little book?) The earliest surviving poetry by Secundus, his fragmentary "In laudem utriusque

---

[1] See Dekker, *Janus Secundus*, 19–20; earlier it had often been assumed that 14 November 1511 was his birthday.

[2] Secundus eulogized him in *Funeral Poems* 7. In line 33, he apostrophized Volcardus as the first to shape his muse: "At tu, Musarum formator prime mearum" (But, oh you who were the first to form my muse).

[3] The dedication, with its strong reminiscences of Catullus 1, was just the thing a schoolmaster would appreciate; the opening of the poem is printed in chapter one (p. 4).

Cupidinis" (In Praise of Each Cupid), was written almost certainly under Stenemola's tutelage.[1] Alfred Dekker suggests that the seventeen metrical Latin translations of epigrams from the *Greek Anthology* (*Epigrams* 2.1–17) may have been school exercises,[2] though it is quite possible that Secundus began this effort later under the influence of Andrea Alciati (who was an early translator of the *Greek Anthology* and Secundus's law professor at Bourges). Stenemola organized the first literary project of the "tres fratres Belgae," a poetic translation of some of Lucian's dialogues.[3] Secundus's efforts were reissued by his brothers in the collected works of 1541 as *Sylvae* 6 and 7.[4] There is, consequently, solid evidence that Secundus left The Hague at the age of seventeen well grounded in Latin stylistics and already devoted to the study of letters and the writing of poetry.

The family moved to Mechlin in September 1528, when Everaerts was named president of the grand council of the Netherlands. By virtue of Margaret of Austria's (1480–1530) residence, Mechlin was a central seat of government for the Netherlands. Secundus resided there initially until he was twenty-one (1532), a period of some four years. This period, moreover, marks the beginning of his mature writing.

As Everaerts's son, he found ready access to the court and, consequently, opportunities to write poetry on political events and for courtly occasions. *Elegies* 3.8 celebrates the peace of Cambrai (August 1529), the famous "Ladies Peace," which Margaret of Austria had negotiated. However, since the poem pays more tribute to Charles than to Margaret, one wonders if it might have been revised later or even written for joint publication with *Odes* 1 (a celebratory ode to Charles V).[5] Secundus also composed two *epicedia* for Margaret after her death on 1 December 1530 (*Funeral Poems* 4 and 5), both of which, as I shall discuss, have traces of amatory poetry.

After Margaret's death and especially during Charles V's residence there (24 January to 28 November 1531), Secundus was frequently in

---

[1] Ellinger, *Geschichte der neulateinischen Literatur*, 3/1:28, places the poem in Secundus's fourteenth or fifteenth year. The fragment is printed in BB, 2:212–16.

[2] See Dekker, *Janus Secundus*, 23.

[3] See ibid., 97–118. Stenemola published his *Luciani libellus* (with poems by Nicolaus Grudius, Hadrianus Marius, and Secundus) in 1530.

[4] Stenemola's book also included Secundus's *Epigrams* 1.37 and 1.38.

[5] Both poems were published together in 1530 in a work by Joannes Dantiscus: *De nostrorum temporum calamitatibus sylva* (Antwerp: Grapheus, 1530).

Brussels (some ten miles south of Mechlin), where he tried very hard, it appears, to win the favor of the imperial court. We find *Odes* 1 on Charles's coronation in Bologna (1530) and *Odes* 6, which welcomes him to Brussels; Secundus also contributed a humorous epigram to the celebration of the emperor's birthday on 24 February 1531 (*Epigrams* 1.21). At this time he also began using his "other art" to impress the court: Secundus sculpted a medallion of Charles, for which he composed a complementary elegy (*Elegies* 3.2).[1] (See fig. 4.) Firm evidence is lacking, but there are many indications that the court welcomed his efforts. After all, two years later, he felt confident enough to journey to the court in Spain without clear prospect of a position. It is perhaps a sign of recognition that Nicolas Gombert († ca. 1556), the court's composer, wrote music for Secundus's *Odes* 10, making it a motet for four voices.[2] Secundus even collaborated with the court's artist Nicolaas Hogenberg († 1539) on two projects. He composed epigrams (*Epigrams* 1.43 and 44) for Hogenberg's set of engravings which were to immortalize Charles V's coronation at Bologna ("De Triomftocht van Karel V en Paus Clemens VII te Bologna").[3] Hogenberg also used *Funeral Poems* 4 and 5, both for Margaret of Austria, for commemorative engravings.[4] Furthermore, Secundus wrote several poems for courtiers and became, for example, a close acquaintance of the poet Joannes Dantiscus (1485–1548), then Polish ambassador to Charles's court.[5]

The Mechlin-Brussels period marked not only his debut as political poet, but also the discovery of his *métier* as a love poet, especially as amatory elegist. In May 1531 he met Julia, a woman of Mechlin,

---

[1] Schoolfield, *Janus Secundus*, 64, supposed that Secundus presented both during his years in Spain. But Dekker's inventory (p. 250) shows that the medallion bears the date 1531.

[2] Dekker, *Janus Secundus*, 40–43, prints Gombert's music.

[3] Ibid., 190–96.

[4] Ibid., 175–90.

[5] See, for example, *Epigrams* 1.45, *Funeral Poems* 19 and 20, *Poetic Epistles* 1.6; at this time he also wrote a poem on the great Zeeland flood of 1530 (*Sylvae* 2) as well as several poetic epistles to Everardus Nicolai (*Poetic Epistles* 1.1, 1.2, 1.3, and 1.4). It is also possible that Jan Gossaert van Mabuse did a portrait of Secundus in Brussels. That depends on the validity of identifying Secundus as the subject of the portrait now hanging in the Staatliche Kunsthalle in Kassel. (See fig. 1.) For a thorough review of the relations between Dantiscus and Secundus, see de Vocht, *John Dantiscus and his Netherlandish Friends*.

to whom some of his best erotic poetry is addressed. According to Secundus's version, he and Petrus Clericus, yet another poet-friend, wooed her.[1] Apparently interested in Secundus initially, she eventually broke off relations with him (and Petrus Clericus) in order to marry a third (unnamed) man. Secundus claims to have left Mechlin for Brussels so as not to witness her wedding to another. Based on Nicolaus Grudius's characterization of her in a letter to Hadrianus Marius and Secundus (29 May 1532), scholars, since 1911, have assumed that the actual Julia was a prostitute.[2] Nonetheless, it is important to note that, aside from Grudius's private letter, there is nothing in Secundus's poetry or in any Renaissance reactions to the *Julia Monobiblos* that suggests this. Thus, as far as Secundus's life and letters are concerned, there is no need to assume that Julia existed and, whether she existed or not, the poetry does not cast her as a prostitute. In addition to composing the elegies, Secundus sculpted a medallion portrait of her—which survives in rather bad condition. (See fig. 5. Moreover, a copy of Jan van Scorel's portrait of Secundus, fig. 2, shows the poet holding a medallion, perhaps one of her.) Whatever the exact nature of the affair may have been, Julia was one of the two important women in his poetry and her elegiac story, whether fictional or based on real experience, became the subject of his first masterpiece. With the exception of *Elegies* 1.2, the *Julia Monobiblos* was completed before Secundus left for Spain. Later, however, he appended three "Elegiae Solemnes" (Ceremonial Elegies) to the collection, written in three successive years as commemorations of his first meeting with her in May 1531.

It is distinctive that, in this first phase, Secundus writes occasionally about art, both visual and literary. To a degree, it is not surprising to find him writing about literature since, owing to the centrality of imitation, Renaissance poetry frequently arises from reflection on earlier literature. Naturally, he writes often of his experience of classical literature, but he also regularly comments on the poetry of Renaissance writers, seeking to connect his own poetry to that of his

---

[1] *Elegies* 1.9 of the *Julia Monobiblos* is addressed to Clericus.

[2] The letter was first published by Molhuysen, "Julia," 107–9. However, Schoolfield, *Janus Secundus*, 91–92, argues for the possibility, while he concedes its unlikelihood, that Julia was not a prostitute. The letter is available in Endres, *Joannes Secundus*, 211–13.

Renaissance forebears and contemporaries. In 1530, as he returned a borrowed book to Franciscus Hoverius, a Mechlin schoolmaster, Secundus recorded his admiration of the erotic poet Michele Marullo[1] and, during the following year in Brussels, composed a tribute to the German poet Joannes Brassicanus († 1539).[2] It is natural, too, that Secundus, as an accomplished sculptor, should write about the visual arts.[3] During this period he finished at least nine medallions (of such subjects as his father, Charles V, Nicolas Perrenot de Granvelle, Dantiscus, and Brassicanus). Secundus prided himself on being the master of a "minor" literary genre—erotic lyric—and it is, indeed, curious that he practiced the minor art of medallion sculpture as well. He usually composed poetry to accompany his medallions, as he did in this period for the medallions of Brassicanus and Charles V; in these poems, he reflected on the idea of commemorative art. The poem to Brassicanus, for example, articulates the humanist cliché that the arts not only commemorate but also immortalize their subject.

On 5 March 1532, Secundus and Hadrianus Marius left Mechlin for Bourges, where they were to study law until late winter 1532, when Secundus received the licentiate degree. The two-week journey to Bourges is described in the prose *Itineraries* 1, which reveals, in particular, Secundus's keen interest in sculpture and architecture. A poem from the itinerary, *Elegies* 3.17, records an encounter with statuary in the abbey-church of St. Denis. Secundus turns his account of the political subjects (the statues are memorials to Charles VIII, his wife Anne de Bretagne, and Louis XII) into a compelling meditation on a connection between life and death in art: "Fictaque stant uno Vitaque Morsque loco" (Both life and death stand fashioned together in one place; *Elegies* 3.17.106). As will be seen, Secundus tends to reflect on the nature of art when he faces a political subject, indicating a hesitancy, I suspect, to admit the larger world of politics into his poetry. Obviously, *Elegies* 3.17 offered a ready topic for the movement away from politics to art, as it is itself a "reading" of political statuary. The finale shows, as we should always expect in Secundus, a thoroughly antique orientation to art. *Imitatio* is a device whereby

---

[1] See *Epigrams* 1.32 and 1.33 (quoted in chapter five).

[2] See *Epigrams* 1.65.

[3] Secundus sometimes refers to himself as a "sculptor-poet," as in *Poetic Epistles* 1.7.9.

art, though for whatever reason inaccessible, lives on in future art as a memory. Praxiteles' "Venus" survives, above all, because antiquity continues to inform sculpture:

> Nimirum digiti vos expoliere Latini;
> Talia barbaricae non potuere manus.
> Vivite dum Cnidiae simulacrum fama Diones
> Praxitelis rarum sera loquetur opus.
> (*Elegies* 3.17.115–18)[1]

[Latin fingers undoubtedly brought you to perfection; barbarian hands could not make such statues. Live on as long as late fame speaks of the image of Cnidean Venus, the rare work of Praxiteles.]

The Bourges year centered mainly around study under Andrea Alciati, perhaps the greatest legal scholar of his day and a poet still remembered as the creator of the emblem book,[2] a genre that gained phenomenal popularity in the sixteenth and seventeenth centuries. In addition to his legal erudition, Alciati was highly regarded for the elegance of his humanist Latin. Erasmus, for example, said that he was the "the most eloquent of the legal scholars."[3] Secundus never failed to praise Alciati's literary accomplishments and it is obvious that the poet-lawyer Secundus was drawn to Alciati for literary as well as scholarly reasons. Upon entering Bourges, Secundus composed an adulatory epigram that associated Alciati's legal expertise with literary skill:

> Magnus ubi Alciatus tanto post tempore primus
> Musarum fidibus Themidis[4] decreta severae
> Aptat, et antiquo revocatur vita Soloni.
> (*Epigrams* 1.59.3–6)

---

[1] Secundus also composed a masterful epigram on the Tour de Nesle and the pathological love of Elisabeth of Bavaria (*Epigrams* 1.72).

[2] Secundus himself wrote a few poems intended, it seems, for emblems; see *Epigrams* 1.4 (on an image of Hercules), 1.42 (on a picture of Icarus), and 1.71 (on a picture about the myth of Phaeton).

[3] Erasmus, *Dialogus Ciceronianus*, 1.2:669: "iurisperitorum eloquentissimus."

[4] "Themidis" is a correction in MS. Rawl. G. 154, fol. 144, for the original "artis."

[Where great Alciati, as the first after a long hiatus, tuned the decrees of severe Themis to the strings of the Muses and where ancient Solon has been revived.]

Epigrams 1.1 compares Alciati, most extravagantly, to Mercury, the humanist god of eloquence. Once again, moreover, Secundus admires the literary style of the legal scholar: "Insuetoque modo mentis decreta severae / Ornat festivi dotibus eloquii" (In a rare fashion, he adorns the decrees of a severe mind with the gifts of genial eloquence; *Epigrams* 1.1.19–20). The association of Alciati with Mercury, I would suggest, is also an allusion to Alciati's *impresa*, which depicted Mercury's caduceus.[1] (See fig. 4 for Secundus's medallion of Alciati.) Secundus even wrote an elegy on Alciati's bout with the plague (*Elegies* 3.9) and, if Dekker is correct, he sent Alciati a poetic epistle on his plans as a law student (*Poetic Epistles* 2.2).[2] *Epigrams* 1.23 is a comic tribute to Alciati which Secundus and Hadrianus Marius, apparently in costume, recited to their professor during Carnival in 1533.

It is perhaps another sign of precocity that, at the age of twenty-one, Secundus qualified for the licentiate's degree after only one year of study, or perhaps it is an indication that the legal preparation received from his father was solid indeed. Moreover, Secundus did not even enjoy an entire year of courses as an outbreak of the plague in the summer of 1532 forced him and his brother to withdraw to Menetou-Salon.

Secundus had already written some funeral poetry for the Hapsburg court (poems for Margaret of Austria and Mercurino di Gattinara). However, several experiences at Bourges and Menetou-Salon compelled him to write funeral poems. While in Menetou-Salon, he learned of his father's death on 9 August 1532 and composed the long tribute that is now *Funeral Poems* 1. In this and other funeral poems, Secundus is preoccupied with the concept of giving the dead a voice beyond the grave. His heavy use of the device of *prosopopeia* informs the theme of life extending beyond death in the form of literary or scholarly monuments. Some of the richness of his funeral poems resides in moments of darkness and fear, yet the overall tone is of a sanguinity built upon confidence in art as a means of transcendence.

---

[1] The verso of Secundus's medallion portrait of Alciati also depicts the caduceus.

[2] Dekker, *Janus Secundus*, 46–47.

Indeed, art—and not Christianity—is the force of salvation in Secundus's poetry. During this period, he also composed epicedial tributes to the French poet Jeanne de la Font (1503–1532), whom he met shortly before her death. He celebrated her *Théséide* (an adaptation of Boccaccio) in *Elegies* 3.15, offering an assurance that, because of this poem, the laurel tree will grow on her grave, conferring the honor that premature death denied. He also composed an *epicedion* (*Funeral Poems* 10) and an epitaph (*Funeral Poems* 11) for her. Both celebrate her more for wifely than poetic qualities,[1] though there are indications that poetry ensures her survival in this world and has vouchsafed her special place in Elysium. The poem about Alciati suffering from the plague (*Elegies* 3.9) also considers the connection between art (and humanist studies) and death, though its tone is less confident. Despite Alciati's mortal weaknesses, he faces death as an artist and his poetic nature allows a special prayer for remission: "sacrum Musis laedere parce caput" (Spare this head consecrated to the Muses; *Elegies* 3.9.10).

In May 1533, Secundus returned to his family in Mechlin. Ready to start his career, but now without the assistance of his powerful father, he decided to join Nicolaus Grudius at the court of Charles V in Spain, apparently hoping that, through his brother's connections, he would be able to secure a position. During his brief stay in Mechlin, he composed two poetic epistles to friends who were aspiring poets: Joachim Polites (*Poetic Epistles* 1.10) and Sybrant Occo (*Poetic Epistles* 1.11). The two letters, both of which mark the occasion of his upcoming departure for Spain, are rambling tributes to their friendship, though occasionally, especially in 1.10, some dark musings on death arise.[2] Such a morbid tone is also heard in *Elegies* 3.10, which was his poetic farewell to friends in the Netherlands, especially to Petrus Clericus and Franciscus Craneveldius; the elegy ends on a maudlin note:

> Vivite felices, dum me tenet ultima tellus,
> Vivite seu vivam, vivite seu moriar.
>
> (*Elegies* 3.10.61–62)

---

[1] In *Funeral Poems* 10, for example, she addresses her grieving husband, encouraging him to allay his sorrow.
[2] See *Poetic Epistles* 1.10.63–74

[Live, fortunate men, as long as the most distant land detains me! Live, whether I live or die!]

Jan van Scorel may have made his first portrait of Secundus shortly before the departure for Spain. The poet reciprocated with a literary tribute (*Poetic Epistles* 2.3) and a *propempticon* (*Epigrams* 1.39). Secundus also wrote a prose letter to Scorel (8 May 1533), asking for a recommendation to Henry III of Nassau, count of Nassau-Dillenburg, who was going to Charles's court in Spain as well.[1] We also learn from the letter that Scorel had expressed admiration for Secundus's medallion of Julia.

Secundus was to spend two years (July 1533–June 1535) in Spain, following the court from La Almunia and Monzón to Saragossa, Toledo, Segovia, Palencia, Madrid, and eventually Barcelona. He continued his efforts to write occasional and political poetry for the court (*Funeral Poems* 9, 13, and 14; *Elegies* 3.12 and 13).[2] He even intended to compose an epic glorification of Charles V's massive expedition against Khair ed-Din Barbarossa († 1547). Though illness stopped Secundus from participating in the campaign, a fragmentary beginning of the *Bellum Tunetanum* (Fragment 2) survives.[3] Secundus did not find a position during his first year in Spain. By June 1534, however, he knew that he would be appointed secretary to Cardinal Juan Pardo de Tavera († 1545), archbishop of Toledo. Schoolfield observes that a letter sent to Everardus[4] shows that Secundus had "become something of an intrigant, determined to succeed in the *vita aulica*."[5] While we know of no intrigues involving Secundus, he unquestionably had visions of his own and his master's elevation.

During the Spanish years, Secundus continued writing amatory poetry, encouraged, no doubt, by the success of his Julia elegies. It was then, perhaps during the court's venue in Toledo (12 February to 21 May 1534), that he met the woman he was to call Neaera. She, too, has been thought to have been a prostitute, though Schoolfield

---

[1] See Letter 2 in BB, 2:272–74.

[2] *Elegies* 3.13 is a *propempticon* for Cardinal Tavera, Secundus's new lord, as he set out for Compostella; Tavera is also celebrated in "Reginae pecuniae regia," which is *Sylvae* 1.

[3] The fragments are printed in BB, 2:212–19.

[4] Letter 3 in BB, 2:274–77.

[5] Schoolfield, *Janus Secundus*, 58.

has demonstrated that the strongest evidence for that assumption has been misunderstood.[1] Some elegies in Book 2 are addressed to her—she is first mentioned, perhaps, in *Elegies* 2.8, which is dated April 1534—but she is most prominent as the beloved of Secundus's *Basia*.[2] *Elegies* 3.13, a *propempticon* to Cardinal Tavera departing for Compostella in the summer of 1534, mentions that Secundus was ill, suffering from fever. Although there is no way of knowing what disease the fever-symptom indicates, some have proposed that syphilis struck down the errant love poet; others have suggested malaria. One thing, though, is certain: complaints of fever are common in the remaining two years of his life.

He departed from Spain in June 1535, his weakened condition having precluded participation in Charles's invasion of Tunis. On the arduous journey home, he again fell seriously ill, which occasioned a two-month stay for recuperation in Poitiers with Cornelius Musius. (Musius, also a poet, would later become the father confessor of Secundus's sister Elisabeth.) In September 1535, he finally arrived in Mechlin, where, after causing his family some initial distress, his condition must have improved considerably. Apparently at the urging of his family, he decided against returning to the service of Tavera. Instead, he quickly got a position as Latin secretary to George van Egmond (1504–1559), the newly named bishop of Utrecht. It was also roughly at this time that Scorel did a second portrait of Secundus, which, though known to have been in the possession of the great poet and Secundus-admirer Constantijn Huygens, is no longer extant.[3]

The poems that can be dated to his last year raise the possibility that political subjects were beginning to take the upper hand over love. That, however, may simply appear to be the case; it is entirely

---

[1] Ibid., 61–62. In *Elegies* 3.16.5–6, Secundus addresses his friend Zurita, "cuique mea ante alios non dedignata Neaera est / Humida adhuc labris basia ferre meis" (to whom, before all others, my Neaera deigned to give her kisses which are still wet from my lips). As Schoolfield astutely notes, this does not indicate that Zurita was a client of Neaera, but rather that he was the first ("ante alios") to read Secundus's *Basia*.

[2] She also plays a role in other poems, such as *Epigrams* 1.34 and *Sylvae* 5 (Secundus's eclogue). There was also another lover in Spain, a certain Venerilla (see *Elegies* 2.2).

[3] An engraving after this portrait appears as the frontispiece to the Burmann-Bosscha edition of Secundus.

possible that, after he returned to the Netherlands, he wrote or revised some of the love poems set in Spain. He composed three *epicedia* for Thomas More, who was beheaded on 6 July 1535 (*Funeral Poems* 26, 27, and 28). The opposition to Henry VIII takes an even more overtly pro-Hapsburg direction in an epitaph for Catherine of Aragon (*Funeral Poems* 29; she died on 7 January 1536).[1] After the dauphin, Francis of Valois, died on 10 August 1536, Secundus wrote an epitaph in opposition to Francis I's invasion of Savoy (February 1536): the dauphin, he says, is fortunate to have died young as he will be spared the consequences of his father's resumption of war (*Funeral Poems* 25). Secundus also impugned the attack on Savoy in two sharp epigrams against Francis (*Epigrams* 1.25 and 1.26).[2]

Sometime in 1536, probably at the end of August or the beginning of September, Secundus received splendid news: Perrenot de Granvelle, Charles V's chancellor, dispatched a letter appointing him a secretary to the emperor. Consequently, he left Mechlin on 13 September 1536 for Saint-Amand, probably in order to settle his affairs with Egmond. He arrived there on 22 September in very bad shape and died three days later on 25 September 1536.

---

[1] Secundus also wrote a poetic letter from Henry VIII to Catherine (*Sylvae* 10).

[2] Another late poem is the *epicedion* to Erasmus (*Funeral Poems* 23), who died on 12 July 1536.

Fig. 4
Medallions by Janus Secundus

Emperor Charles V (recto and verso)
Bronze; 46 mm
Reproduced courtesy of Koninklijke Bibliotheek Albert I

Andrea Alciati (recto and verso)
Bronze; 41 mm
Reproduced from L. Simonis,
L'Art du médailleur en Belgique (1900), plate 3

3   Writing Love: The Amatory Elegy as Poetology

Cui damus hos Elegos? tibi, qui legis ista libenter,
  Cui micat in laeta fronte serena Venus.
Seria qui curas, procul hinc age seria, ferri
  Nos sine, quo Pueri iura volantis agunt.
    Secundus, *Elegies* 2.1.1–4

[To whom do I dedicate these elegies? To you, since you read
them with pleasure and because serene Venus glows on your
happy brow. But you who trouble yourself about worldly matters ("serious things"), drive worldly matters away from these
verses, let me be transported to where the laws of the winged
boy obtain.]

Despite the author's plea, scholars have taken the *Elegies* seriously
enough to rank them among the most important Latin poetry of the
Renaissance. There is an informal consensus among the critics, it seems,
that of the northern European elegists Secundus's only peer is Petrus
Lotichius (1528–1560). Altogether, Secundus's three books of elegies
contain just forty-three poems: eleven in Book One; eleven in Book
Two; eighteen in Book Three; and three "Elegiae Solemnes" (Celebratory Elegies), which have been appended to Book One. The organization of the elegies into books derives at least in part from the author.
Book One (which, as the most important collection, will be the focus of
my discussion) is the *Julia Monobiblos*, a cycle of amatory poems for a
woman with the literary sobriquet of Julia. Most of the cycle was
completed during the Mechlin-Brussels period (1528–1532), though
Secundus inserted *Elegies* 1.2 into the cycle in 1534.[1]
  Book Two would appear to have been organized by the poet. It has

---

[1] That the insertion of *Elegies* 1.2 dates from 1534 is certain from a letter to
Hadrianus Marius which is dated 3 June 1534; see BB, 2:277–78.

a discrete proemium in which he dedicates the elegies to his brothers
Nicolaus Grudius and Hadrianus Marius (who were, of course, to
become the editors of the *editio princeps* of the *Elegies*). Furthermore,
the uniform theme is love, though, unlike Book One, Book Two
contains poems on several women (most notably *Elegies* 2.5, which is
addressed to Neaera) and even an epithalamium to Nicolaus Grudius on
the occasion of his second marriage (*Elegies* 2.10).

While Book Three also has a proemium, it is a miscellany of elegies on subjects other than love, though *Elegies* 3.1 and 3.3 do discuss
love poetry.[1] One is left with the impression that the brothers may
have organized Books Two and Three, or that they may have inserted amatory poems into an inchoate Book Two and gathered the elegies on other subjects into Book Three. The *Elegies*, I should add, do
not include all the poems Secundus composed in elegiac distich (i.e.,
alternating lines of hexameter and pentameter to form couplets).
Book One of the *Poetic Epistles*, many of the *Basia*, *Epigrams* and
Funeral Poems, as well as *Sylvae* 6, 7, and 10 are written in distich.

The *Elegies* have given rise to considerable speculation on Secundus's actual love affairs and, similarly, have provided the basis for
earlier scholars to muse on the Romantic ideal of experience inform-
ing art or giving it authenticity. No scholar, though, has failed to remark on the importance of convention in Secundus's aesthetic—indeed, all admit the need to assess his imitation of ancient authors.[2]
Monologic interpretations of individual imitations, though, can be
badly misleading. Clifford Endres and Barbara Gold, for example, offer a highly selective reading of Secundus's imitation of two passages
in Ovid and Propertius to support a view that Secundus "rejects the
essence of poetry itself."[3] Their argument, which seeks, perhaps unconsciously, to reposition the concept of "Erlebnis" in the analysis
of the *Elegies* (used so reductively by Ellinger in his biographical ap-

---

[1] Though not universal, a distinctive theme of Book Three is art. Six poems
(*Elegies* 3.3, 3.4, 3.7, 3.15, 3.16, and 3.17) are addressed to poets and two others
(*Elegies* 3.5 [on a falsely announced return of Erasmus to the Netherlands] and 3.9
[on Alciati's bout with plague]) are addressed to literary figures.

[2] It is only fair to emphasize that the Burmann-Bosscha edition is the source
of all studies of Secundus's relationship to his sources. While I and other
scholars may identify a few additional sources, we remain profoundly indebted
to Burmann-Bosscha.

[3] Endres and Gold, "Joannes Secundus and his Roman Models," 589.

proach), proposes that Secundus is interested in love and that he rejects love poetry as a viable interest or even as a source of inspiration.[1] This, *prima facie*, is not persuasive since the elegies reflect constantly on poetics. That he remarks on its inefficaciousness does not indicate by itself a rejection of amatory poetry. In fact, his excessive literariness derives from the association of both desire and literature (or art) as sources of experience.

Elegies 3.1, the evidence for the argument of Endres and Gold, certainly does impugn the futility of poetry. What can poetry accomplish in the real world? As noted by Burmann and Bosscha, the elegy is strongly reminiscent of a passage from Ovid (*Amores* 2.1.23ff.) and has slight overtones of Propertius (3.2.3–4 and 4.5). The passages from Propertius and, especially, Ovid occur in poems that reaffirm the validity of elegiac art—something that the first fourteen lines of *Elegies* 3.1 only *appear* to do. Secundus begins with an excessively emphatic (is it self-parodistic?), seven-fold anaphora of "carminibus" which conveys the apparent miracles Orpheus accomplished "with songs." A *volta* at line 15 ("Sed *non* carminibus") revokes the wonderment expressed in lines 1–14, asserting that Orpheus, after all, did not succeed in resurrecting Eurydice. As will be seen in the *Basia* and *Epigrams*, Secundus often uses such an antithetical structure to achieve an ironic effect.[2] After the *volta*, the remainder of the poem contrasts the power of "munera" (money or gifts) with the impotence of songs.[3] While Secundus's persona is cynical and disillusioned, it is not bitter or troubled. In fact, he trivializes the dominance of money by citing humorous evidence from "revised" mythology. Danae, he claims, was not interested in love letters, but in the gold which poured into her lap.[4] His humor reaches a sort of epigrammatic *pointe* in the apostrophe to Penelope that ends the poem:

> Munera fecissent cunctos ex ordine sponsos
> Participes thalami, Penelopea, tui;

---

[1] Ibid., 586: "He puts emphasis on the *calor* itself, stressing the power of love rather than the rhetorical power of poetry."

[2] Endres, *Joannes Secundus*, 50, inappropriately states "he is seldom epigrammatic or antithetical in Ovid's manner."

[3] Secundus also wrote a satire on money and wealth, "Reginae pecuniae regia" (*Sylvae* 1), which, with 264 lines, is his longest poem.

[4] Though Secundus's point is quite different, he may be thinking of Horace, *Odes* 3.16, here.

Sed non dona dabant, vel si tibi dona dederunt,
   Falsa tuae fertur fama pudicitiae.
                              (*Elegies* 3.1.37–40)

[Penelope, money would have given all the suitors, in order, access to your bed. But they gave no gifts—or if they did, your
reputation for chastity is a myth.]

Elegies 3.1 has been called a "repudiation" of the ancient elegists'
faith in their genre, but nothing could be farther from the case. The
ironization of both parts of the antithesis of "carmina" and "munera" makes the poem, above all, a *jeu d'esprit*. Moreover, the ironization of love poetry, while it does stand, strategically perhaps, at the
beginning of the book of elegies unconcerned with love, conforms
nonetheless to Secundus's overall pattern of contrasting the light,
trivial subjects of amatory poetry with the serious concerns of political life, and qualifying that contrast with irony. He undermines the
high-flying tribute to the power of poetry to evoke a sense of nugatory poetics—the ideal of writing poetry that does not matter in any
ordinary political or social sense. Moreover, Secundus had (and
knew) many classical precedents for bemoaning the inefficiency of
love poetry, especially when it competes with the attractiveness of
wealth. Burmann and Bosscha cite Ovid, *Amores* 2.275ff., Tibullus
2.4.14ff. and Propertius 2.13.15ff. In fact, not at all a repudiation,
Elegies 3.1 is a humorous treatment of what is itself a topos of ancient
elegy: the poor poet offering only songs hasn't got a chance. *Elegies*
3.1 need not be read as a rejection of love poetry, but rather as an ex-
ploration of the elegy's potential for jest, whereby it evokes a Catullan epigrammatic, as well as an Ovidian antithetical, style.

   Though some poems are informed by an apologetic theory of imitation, much of Secundus's *imitatio* in the *Elegies* has a practical aspect of
style. He had completely, it seems, absorbed the Roman corpus of love
elegies (not to mention odes, epigrams, and satires). Consequently, he
wrote distichs that were rich in literary resonance, even when he was
not quoting or parodying a particular Roman author. It is almost certain
that he had committed enormous amounts of Latin poetry to memory,
enabling him, as Secundus himself stresses, to write poetry with the
"mollia verba" (gentle words) of the Romans.

   Although he never repudiates ancient convention, he can adopt a
playful attitude toward the classics. In *Elegies* 3.3, he composes an
"eroticized" tribute to Catullus, Tibullus, and Propertius, the poets

who, in addition to Ovid, exerted the greatest influence on the *Elegies*[1]:

> Intemerata vides linguae monumenta Latinae,
> Delicias dominae, lautitiasque togae.
> Scilicet hic omne est, colles audire Quirini
> Molle vel argutum quod potuere prius.
> Hic et Pompeia spatiaris serus in umbra,
> Subque tuos oculos multa puella venit,
> Laxa comam, religata comam, distincta capillum,
> Culta, nigris oculis, crine decora nigro.
> Inter quas prima procedit[2] Lesbia pompa,
> Passeris interitu nunc quoque moesta sui.
> Totque tibi blando promittit basia vultu,
> Lenis amatori quot dedit ante suo.
> Proxima progreditur lascivo[3] Delia passu,
> Felicem Nemesis quam prope radit humum.
> Fortunatae ambae, quarum sacra fama virebit,
> Pectora dum vatum parvus aduret Amor.
> Cynthia deinde potens oculis, iaculantibus ignem,
> Subsequitur[4] Coa mobilis in tunica.
> Haec domuit fortem, tactumque Cupidine nullo,
> Et fastus spolium celsa tuentis habet.
> Tu quoque, qui cernis, cave ne laedaris ab illa,
> Spirat adhuc flammas, et sua tela gerit.
>
> (*Elegies* 3.3)

[Here you see the undefiled monuments of the Latin language, the delights[5] of the mistress, the elegance of the toga. Herein is, indeed, all the tender and witty poetry the hills of Rome have

---

[1] There are, however, also many traces of Vergil and Horace in the *Elegies*, even though they were not elegists.

[2] MS. Rawl. G. 154, fol. 64, has "procedit" as a correction of the crossed out "spaciatur."

[3] Ibid., fol. 64, has "progreditur lascivo" as a correction of the crossed out "composito procedit." Obviously, this change was necessitated by the change to "procedit" in line 9.

[4] Ibid., fol. 64, has "subsequitur" as a correction for the crossed out "progreditur," a change necessitated by the alteration made in line 13.

[5] "Delicias" also has the meaning of "erotic poems."

ever heard. Here you walk at night in the Portico of Pompey and many women pass by your eyes—some have let their hair down, others put it up, others have decorated it—they are elegant and beautiful with dark eyes and dark hair. In the parade goes Lesbia, though now saddened by the death of her sparrow. And she promises you as many kisses with her beautiful mouth as the gentle woman previously gave her lover. Delia comes next with a sexy walk and, next to her, Nemesis touches the blessed earth. Both are blessed whose holy fame will grow as long as little Cupid ignites the hearts of poets. Thereupon follows Cynthia, gliding in her silk robe, powerful with her eyes casting fire. She mastered a brave man, never touched by love; and aloft she holds the spoils of her defensive pride. You, too, you who gaze on this, make sure she does not wound you. She still emits flames and still carries her weapons.]

Though the poem is a tribute to the Roman eroticists and though its language evokes the Augustan elegy, Secundus's direct imitations are limited to the descriptions of Cynthia (which is taken from Propertius 1.2.2 and 1.1.1–4) and the Portico of Pompey.[1] The markers of ancient poetry are otherwise more obvious than usual: Lesbia with her sparrow (Catullus 2 and 3) as well as her kisses (Catullus 5 and 7); Delia (heroine of Tibullus's Book One) and Nemesis (heroine of Tibullus's Book Two); and, as mentioned, Propertius's Cynthia, who seems to have stepped out of Propertius 1.1. The poem may document a debt to ancient style and language, but it also reveals a distinctive aspect of Secundus's reception of the ancients and his stylization of amatory verse. The veracity of erotic poetry is never an issue; what matters is that it creates an experience of love. Schoolfield's remark that Secundus seems more interested in the women than in the poets (a remark that is itself true to Secundus's irony) is a witty way of drawing attention to the idea that poetry creates experience. Secundus is keenly interested in both love and literature, so much so that he postulates an experience of love—albeit humorously—in his parade of famous leading ladies from literature, a device he also uses in *Elegies* 3.16.[2] The experience, though, remains rooted in a literary

---

[1] There are at least three sources for this: Ovid, *Ars amatoria* 65; Martial 11.47; and Propertius 4.8.75.

[2] *Elegies* 3.16 is addressed to the Saragossan poet Jerónimo de Zurita. The

sense throughout and consequently suggests an elusive ideal. For example, when Delia comes with "sexy walk" ("lascivo ... passu"), the Latin text evokes a literary sense: "lascivo passu" could also mean an elegy "in the erotic meter" (a reference to elegiac distich)—just as it describes an alluring movement off the literary page.[1]

The *Julia Monobiblos* expresses a complex attitude toward imitation and literary tradition. In a rather general sense, the *Julia Monobiblos* was inspired by Propertius's first book of elegies, the *Cynthia Monobiblos*. Perhaps even more so than Propertius, Secundus gives his cycle tight formal coherence. After a proemium, which introduces the genre of amatory elegy, the poems provide a rough chronology of the affair, broken off by Julia's engagement (*Elegies* 1.7) and marriage (*Elegies* 1.8) to a rival and Secundus's departure for Brussels (*Elegies* 1.9). The collection as a whole also imbricates a set of consistent motifs, most of which are strongly reminiscent of ancient poetry.[2]

In some way, each poem engages in a metadiscourse with antiquity, but two poems evince a distinctively playful attitude toward ancient art (*Elegies* 1.6 and 1.9). In *Elegies* 1.6, which is also interesting because it records a real event in Secundus's career as a sculptor, he invokes the support of ancient artists in an attempt to sculpt a medallion of Julia. (See fig. 5 for the actual medallion of Julia by Secundus.)

> Nunc mihi Praxitelis digiti, nunc Mentoris essent,
>   Nunc Lysippeae, Phidiacaeque manus!
> Iulia namque meo sculpi[3] cupit aurea caelo,
>   Nec tantum in libris nomen habere meis.
> Non ego sum, fateor, coelestem effingere[4] formam

---

idea that literature is experience informs Secundus's description of Zurita getting Neaera's kisses (i.e., the kiss poems) in lines 5–6. See lines 31–34 for another parade of women from ancient elegy, where, unlike *Elegies* 3.3, Ovid's Corinna is included.

[1] I must stress, though, that "lascivo" is an emendation of the original text of MS. Rawl. G. 154. That probably means that "lascivo" is the formulation of the brothers.

[2] Sometimes a motif in Secundus simultaneously recalls several ancient authors. See, for example, *Elegies* 1.4.21–24, which evokes Ovid, *Heroides* 4.47–48, Catullus 61.33–35 and Horace, *Epodes* 15.5–6.

[3] MS. Rawl. G. 154, fol. 26, has "sculpi" as a correction for the crossed out "fingi" (?).

[4] Ibid., fol. 26, "effingere" replaces the crossed out "sculpere," a change necessitated by the alteration to line 3.

Qui valeam; at dominae spernere iussa nefas.
Non ego te, mea lux, faciam de marmore duro;[1]
Illa decet rigidum materies animum.
Quin et caela tuos formabunt aurea vultus;
Non facit ad molles ferrea lima genas.
Iam iam fama meis maior venit artibus; ipsam
Sculpere mi videor coelicolam Venerem.
Sed dum te video, et propius tua lumina specto,
Aemula Phoebeis lumina luminibus,
Ferre negant oculi iaculantem spicula vultum,
Coelaque nota negat languida ferre manus.
Deficit et torpet, nec iam sibi conscius artis
Ullius est animus, nec memor ipse sui.
Ah! nulli fas est mortali effingere Divas.
Mens cadit: obstupeo, heu! et mihi surripior!

(*Elegies* 1.6)

[If I now had the fingers of Praxiteles and Mentor as well as the hands of Lysippus and Phidias! For golden Julia wishes to be sculpted by my chisel—it's not enough for her to have her name in my book. But, I confess, I am not the one who can capture that heavenly beauty. But it is sacrilege to refuse the mistress's orders.

My dear, I shouldn't fashion you of hard marble as that medium suits an unyielding spirit. Rather, golden chisels will shape your features; the iron file doesn't work for soft cheeks. Now! Now a greater fame is entering my veins; I seem to be sculpting heavenly Venus herself.

But when I see you and look at your eyes more closely, eyes that rival Apolline lights, my eyes cannot endure your visage casting darts, and my hand, now languid, cannot hold the familiar chisels. My spirit contracts and is paralyzed, unaware of any art, forgetful of itself. Oh, it is sacrilege for a mortal to depict the gods. My mind is collapsing, I'm silent, alas, I am being stolen away from myself.]

---

[1] Ibid., fol. 26, line 7 is a correction for the original, crossed out phrase "Non ego te duro, mea Lux, e marmore fingam."

With typically self-conscious preciosity, Secundus delicately asserts that for a moment—for a single line (*Elegies* 1.6.11: "fama maior")— his art can achieve a fame greater than that of antiquity. The amatory-poetic paradox, though, is light-hearted: Julia transports his art beyond that of the Greeks, but her beauty overwhelms him, stymieing his art. Though without a quote, the poem suggest Catullus's famous translation of Sappho (Catullus 51: "Ille me par esse deo videtur"). Catullus's "fas" ("Ille, si fas est, superare divos") may inform Secundus's use of "nefas" and "fas," though a link between Catullus 51 and *Elegies* 1.6 is established mainly by the general image of incapacitation. Secundus, however, suggests an even more profound loss of self and connects it, most subtly, to a disorientation from ancient art. *Elegies* 1.5 similarly suggests an amatory transcendence of ancient models as Julia has the potential for surpassing the women of ancient elegy: "Exsuperas Latias et tamen ore nurus" (Yet you surpass the Roman women with your beauty; *Elegies* 1.5.30).

The idea of amatory competition ("aemulatio") with ancient culture also informs *Elegies* 1.9, a letter written from Brussels to his friend Petrus Clericus, who had stayed behind in Mechlin. According to the poem, Brussels is the recreation of antiquity: it is the site of imperial dignity[1]; it supports a crowd of great poets; its sculpture is so magnificent that it induces the poet to experience visions of men dressed in togas. In fact, Brussels rivals the culture of both Greece and Rome: "Scilicet argutis urbs haec me ponit Athenis; / Scilicet hic media sistor in Ausonia" (Indeed, this city transports me to tuneful Athens; indeed, I am planted in the midst of Ausonia; lines 13–14). However, the poem turns, once again antithetically, in lines 15–16: "Mille vel hic oculos possunt retinere, vel aures / Nulla tenent aures, nulla tenent oculos" [Here, a thousand things are able to hold either my eyes or my ears—none of them holds my ears, none of them holds my eyes]. The *volta* moves away from classical Brussels to contemplation of the love recently lost in Mechlin. The structural antithesis between Brussels and Mechlin locates the poet, somewhat disoriented, between antiquity and his love. Naturally, this acknowledges his debt to antiquity, but he is compelled to turn away from the ancient world as he is drawn to his own love or love poetry. And yet, in his distress, he wishes that Venus, as a cipher for ancient love

---

[1] In *Elegies* 1.9.3, Charles V is simply called "Augustus."

poetry, might save Julia for him, knowing, however, the hopelessness of his appeal to antiquity.[1]

Secundus introduces the *Julia Monobiblos* with a kind of *recusatio*, a "refusal" to write epic, and a declaration of allegiance to the "trivial" art of the love elegy.

Pierides alius dira inter[2] bella cruentet,
    Vulneraque ingeminet saeva, necesque virum,[3]
Cuius bis fuso madefiant sanguine versus:
    Hei mihi, plus satis est quem cecidisse semel.
Nos Puerum sancta volucrem cum Matre canamus,
    Spargentem tenera tela proterva manu.
Sic ego: sic fanti radiantibus adstitit alis,
    Cum face, cum cornu, cum iaculisque Puer.
Fallor? an ardentes acuebat cote sagittas?
    Anxius in vultu iam mihi pallor erat.
Parce tuum, dixi, ferro terrere poetam,
    Castra parat dudum qui tua sponte sequi,
Imperiumque potens, et regna patentia late,
    Quae te spumigena cum genitrice colunt:
Carmine vocali patrias resonare per urbes
    Aggreditur: tuus est; laedere parce tuum.
Ille nihil motus, lunato fervidus arcu,
    Accipe quae, dixit, multa diuque canas:
Et non ignotae celebra nunc robora dextrae;
    Formaque quid valeat disce decentis herae.
Vix ea personuit, sonuit simul arcus, et una
    Cum iaculo in venas sensimus isse Deum.

[Let another bloody the Muses in harsh wars and reiterate the savage wounds and slaughter of men. Let his poetry drip with blood twice shed. Alas, for me it is more than enough to have died once. Let me sing of the boy flying with his holy mother, scattering wicked missiles with his gentle hand.

---

[1] Secundus ends *Elegies* 1.9 in lines 45–52 with *aprosdochesis* (i.e., an unexpected conclusion): he now longs to return to Mechlin because another woman ("Domitilla") will have sex with him there.

[2] MS. Rawl. G. 154, fol. 1, "dira inter" is a correction of the crossed out "inter fera."

[3] Ibid., fol. 1, "virum" is a correction for a crossed out, illegible word; it appears to be a form of "vir."

Thus I spoke. And as I spoke thus, the boy stood before me with his flashing wings—with a torch, bow, and arrows. What's that? Am I mistaken, or was he sharpening some fiery arrows on a whetstone?[1] In my distress, my face blenched. I said: "Don't threaten your poet with iron. Just now he is preparing to enter your army voluntarily and to make his native cities resound in tuneful poetry with praise of your mighty empire and the immense realms that worship you and your mother, born from the sea-spray. He is yours. Don't harm your poet."

Not at all moved, eagerly bending his curved bow, he said: "Receive many things which you can sing of for a long time. Celebrate the powers of my right arm, now that you have experienced them. Learn how powerful a charming mistress's beauty can be." Scarcely had he rung his message when the bow rang out and, at once, I felt, with the arrow, that a god had entered my veins.]

Elegies 1.1, the proemium to Secundus's first book of mature poetry, introduces a theme that will recur throughout his oeuvre: valorization of the apolitical erotic poem over the political epic. As shown by the vivid image of the page being bloodied by martial epic, the poem also introduces the concept that literature is a form of experience. (Indeed, according to the poem, an epic spills blood a second time.) In the elevation of the amatory poetics to the status of epic, Secundus, obviously operating in the Ovidian realm of "militat omnis amans" (every lover goes to war [or: does battle]), describes love with militaristic metaphors. This characteristic, which occurs often in his poetry,[2] always suggests a stylistic shift to the mock-heroic, though with varying degrees of humor or irony. The faux-heroic voice, which is also used in ancient elegy, both elevates, by way of gesture, the "trivial" genre and parodies—and hence lowers—the serious style and matter of epic. That love is war can deepen the image of the lover suffering, deprived and wounded, but it also, more importantly, articulates opposition to a concept of politically meaningful poetry. In *Elegies* 1.2, which elaborates on the apolitical program of 1.1, Secundus even receives an explicit caveat from Cupid: (Nil tibi

---

[1] This is an echo of Horace, *Odes* 2.8.15–16.

[2] It reappears in the *Julia Monobiblos*, for example, in the final elegy (1.11).

sit) "cantare tui victricia Caesaris arma" (You are not to sing of the victorious arms of your Caesar; *Elegies* 1.2.91). Study of the "empire ... and kingdom"[1] of Cupid (*Elegies* 1.1.12ff.) is, then, an alternative to the military might of Caesar. Naturally, there is considerable irony in Cupid's "defeat" of the poet in *Elegies* 1.1 as he defends his aesthetic. The entire poem, though, focuses on poetic aesthetic. On a mundane level, the first line obviously evokes Tibullus 1.1.1 ("Divitias alius fulvo sibi congerat auro" [let someone else pile up riches in golden heaps]), but changes Tibullus's concern for an ethic of life into a poetological statement ("let someone else bloody the Muses").[2] The finale, moreover, speaks to the issue of writing inspired poetry—the god's injection into Secundus's veins recalls the idea of the much quoted lines from Ovid's *Fasti* that inspiration is the presence of the divine ("Est deus in nobis" [There is a god in us; *Fasti* 6.5]). The metadiscourse on poetics is most articulate when Cupid threatens the poet. When Secundus hears love speak, he actually hears the words of Ovid:

"Accipe quae," dixit, "multa diuque canas"

["Receive many things," he said, "which you can sing of for a long time."]

is taken directly from:

"Quod," que, "canas, vates, accipe," dixit, "opus."

[And he (i.e., Cupid) said, "Poet, receive a work of which you can sing."]

The words of love—amatory poetry—are the words of Ovid. But, most importantly, Secundus construes the concept of imitation as one aspect of his reading of love poetry as experience. As this and other poems illustrate, reading literature becomes an experience of love. Thus, according to Secundus, the source of eros can be a confluence of experience and literary tradition, just as writing love poetry becomes an amatory act.

---

[1] Derived from Ovid, *Amores* 1.13.

[2] See also Tibullus's anti-war poem (1.10). While Tibullus writes against war itself, Secundus writes against poems about war.

The analogy of love to political poetry is not limited to *Elegies* 1.1 and 1.2. Several subsequent poems appropriate the language of government, law, and war. In *Elegies* 1.7, for instance, it is the "lady" ("domina") who "rules" the poet. In 1.7.31, he claims, as she is about to leave him to marry, that "you could have ruled me with regal words and possessed a sublime kingdom in my verse."[1] In *Elegies* 1.3, we find the first sustained formulation of the idea that beauty is power (though there are hints of that already in *Elegies* 1.1),[2] which was to become a leitmotif of the nugatory poetics and find its classic formulation in the famous line from *Basia* 8, "O vis superba formae" (Oh proud power of beauty). Moreover, in *Elegies* 1.3, the beloved is a "victrix" who has conquered the poet; she legislates laws ("leges"); has the trappings of political authority ("sceptra"); and above all possesses empire ("imperium").

> Illa mihi leges victrix praescribat, et in me
> Regia formosis sceptra gerat manibus.
>
> > (*Elegies* 1.3.23–24)

[Let her, the conqueror, dictate laws for me and let her hold royal scepters in her beautiful hands with power over me.]

A corollary to the appropriation of political language is inversion of the values of political life: poverty is superior to wealth; defeat preferable to victory; personal more important than public world; and the slight lyric better than the exalted epic. Art becomes the force that can achieve the inversion of the political-personal hierarchy. A recurring message is the exaltation of the low. When love is favorable, "humble cottages surpass haughty mansions" ([sub amore secundo …] "Et vincunt humiles tecta superba casae"[3]). The deflation of the political sphere is consequently the *pointe* of Secundus's hopeful *Elegies* 1.4:

> At vos, purpurei reges, ignoscite victi,
> Risus erunt vestrae tunc mihi divitiae.
>
> > (lines 25–26)

---

[1] See *Elegies* 1.7.31–34 (quoted below in note 38).

[2] See *Elegies* 1.3.9: "Formae … potentis" and the subsequent repetitions of "formosa."

[3] One thinks, here, of Corydon's plea to Alexis in Vergil, *Eclogues* 2.26.

[As for you, kings in purple, be indulgent when you have been conquered. Then I shall laugh at your wealth.]

Scorning wealth may sound like an echo of Tibullus, but Secundus also uses the topos to rebuff the world of politics. A similar binary opposition informs Secundus's dream-poem where he asserts that others may dream of wealth, but he shall dream of her (see *Elegies* 1.10, quoted below).

There are also indications that "lawlessness" is an ideal. In *Elegies* 1.7, a rival appears for Julia's affection, who, unlike Secundus, promises marriage—with its laws and strictures. Secundus henceforth uses the motif of the Golden Age not so much as an emblem of pacifism or anti-materialism, but as a utopian concept of love without law. Thus, in addition to the successful rival, Hymen becomes, as the god of marriage, an object of Secundus's invective in three separate poems (*Elegies* 1.7, 1.8, and 1.11). A passage in *Elegies* 1.7 emphasizes the liberty of the paradise lost and the cruelty of the age that followed.

> Quam bene priscorum currebat vita parentum,
>   Ingenuae Veneris libera sacra colens!
> Nondum coniugii nomen servile patebat,
>   Nec fuerat Divis adnumeratus Hymen.
> Passim communes exercebantur amores
>   Omnibus, et proprii nescius orbis erat.
> Ense maritali nemo confossus adulter
>   Purpureo Stygias sanguine tinxit aquas.
> Anxia non tenuit custodis cura puellam,
>   Nulla erat invisis clausa domus foribus;
> Nec sacer agricolis stabat lapis arbiter agro,
>   Trabsque procellosum nulla secabat iter.
> At postquam domibusque fores, foribusque subivit
>   Clavis, et aequoreas navita sprevit aquas,
> Non dubitans animam tenui concredere ligno,
>   Externas fragili puppe secutus opes,[1]
> Discretique novo iacuerunt limite campi,
>   Indixit leges et sibi quisque novas;
> Scilicet ex illo sensit fera iura, iacetque

---

[1] MS. Rawl. G. 154, fol. 18, "opes" is a correction for the crossed out "aquas."

Clausa pedem dura compede serva Venus.
Mortales, sceleri leges praescribite[1] vestro,
Innocuam vinclis nec cohibete Deam.
(*Elegies* 1.7.65–86)

[How good the life of our forebears was when they worshipped
the free rites of free-born Love. Not yet was the slavish name of
marriage known, nor was Hymen counted among the gods. All
over, everyone enjoyed communal loves; the world was igno-
rant of individual love. No adulterer, gouged by a husband's
sword, stained the Styx's waters with bright blood. The girl
didn't worry about gatekeepers. The house wasn't locked with
hated bolts. Nor did a sacred stone stand on the field as a mark-
er to the farmers. No ship cut a stormy journey on the sea.

But after houses got doors and doors got locks and the sailor
scoffed at the ocean's waters, unconcerned about entrusting his
life to the slight bark, pursuing foreign wealth in a fragile ship
and the fields lay marked out by new boundaries, then each area
legislated new laws for itself.

Indeed, from that time on, enslaved love felt savage laws and
she lies enchained, her foot in hard shackles. Humankind, pre-
scribe laws for your own wickedness, do not confine an innocent goddess with chains.]

The Golden Age eschews marriage but also expresses a more general
concept of lawlessness. The intensity of this poem's rhetoric not only
defines the restrictions and confinements of law, but also makes the
constriction sound (or feel) so tight as to be about to snap. Restric-
tion has an overtly violent quality here and, above all, the general
sense that government and law put the human spirit of love in
shackles. The utopia of the Golden Age dissociates love from law, al-
legorically endorsing, in turn, a concept of poetics unconstrained by
convention. The Secundian ideal would exclude the public realm
from taking possession of his poetry since poetry must remain un-
bound by strictures of law or custom.[2]

---

[1] Ibid., fol. 18, "leges praescribite" is a correction for the crossed out
"poenam decernite."

[2] See also Secundus, *Odes* 5, which develops the theme of marriage as slavery
in a similar fashion.

Marriage and poetry are also connected in *Elegies* 1.8, where Apollo, god of poetry, answers Secundus's prayer for bad weather on Julia's wedding day. Critics have fittingly dubbed 1.8 an anti-epithalamium. He continues to appropriate political language to describe marriage (in line 7 Julia is said to be entering into pacts ["foedera"] with a foreigner) and the institution of marriage remains a form of slavery:

> Ergo dies venit, qua se formosa mariti
> Dedit in aeternum Iulia servitium.
>
> *(Elegies* 1.8.1–2)

[Thus the day has come on which beautiful Julia has given herself to the eternal slavery of a husband.]

Interestingly, Secundus is also famous as the author of another epithalamium, printed by the brothers as *Sylvae* 8.[1] This epithalamium, however, is ultimately unlike any wedding poem from the Renaissance as it does not celebrate the social function of matrimony—indeed, there is not even the slightest clue as to whom it may have been written for. Rather, it extols the pleasures of love and sex, free from societal (or poetic) constraints. In fact, Secundus uses the epithalamium as a device for celebrating his nugatory poetics. Thus the moment of the wedding is described with language used to characterize his amatory aesthetic:

> Hora suavicula et voluptuosa,
> Hora blanditiis, lepore, risu,
> Hora deliciis, iocis, susurris,
> Hora suaviolis, . . .
>
> *(Sylvae* 8.1–4)

[The hour sweet and sexy, the hour for love talk, charm, jest, the hour for delights, play, and whispers, the hour for little kisses . . .]

---

[1] As a favorite poem in Secundus's oeuvre, the epithalamium is widely available. Maurice Rat translated it into French (Secundus, *Les baisers*, 36–45) and Nichols included it in his brief selection of Secundus's works (*An Anthology of Neo-Latin Poetry*, 514–23). The love poet Johann Christian Günther also translated it into German in the early eighteenth century, an effort Schoolfield, *Janus Secundus*, 134, called a "fiasco."

It is also reminiscent of the elegies that, in the epithalamium, Secundus uses military language, though only after stripping it of political meaning; moreover, he uses poetic license to portray sexual intercourse vividly, perhaps so vividly as to offend moralistic literary sensibilities:

> Tunc arma expedienda, tunc ad arma
> Et Venus vocat, et vocat Cupido:
> Tunc in vulnera grata proruendum.
> Huc illuc agilis feratur hasta,
> Quam crebro furibunda verset ictu
> Non Martis soror, sed amica Martis
> Semper laeta novo cruore Cypris.
> Nec quies lateri laborioso
> Detur, mobilibus nec ulla coxis:
> Donec deficiente voce anhela,
> Donec deficientibus medullis,
> Membris languidulis, madens uterque
> Sudabit varii liquoris undas.
> O noctem nimis, o nimis beatam!
>
> (*Sylvae* 8.122–35)

[Then arms must be readied. Then Venus calls you to arms and Cupid calls, too. Then rush forward to receive the pleasing wounds. Here and there may the fast spear be thrust; not the raging sister of Mars, let the lover of Mars, Venus, who always enjoys the fresh blood, drive it with repeated thrusts. Nor should the laboring thighs rest, not the moving hips, until with failing, heaving panting, and with failing hearts and languid limbs, each of you, wet, will exude streams of different fluid,— oh much too, oh much too happy night!]

The closing poem of the *Julia Monobiblos* also attributes a utopian lawlessness to the Golden Age and places social stricture in a binary opposition to poetry. But, here, Secundus expresses his poetic ideal in a characteristically sensual image of "nude" poetry, as he challenges his rival to leave Julia untouched, but, instead, to "look to" the muses:

> Nonne fuit satius cantus haurire sororum,
>   Cernere vel, sacrae qua fluit humor aquae,
> Veste Deas posita teretes abscondere suras,
>   Quam miseram turpi dedere servitio?
>
> (*Elegies* 1.11.27–30)

[Would it not have been more satisfying to drink in the songs of the Muses or even to watch them, where the wetness of the sacred water flows, dip their well-rounded calves, after having removed their clothing, rather than to have thrust the pitiful woman into wicked slavery?]

In addition to sensualizing the idea of freedom, this passage proposes, to the rival, that love must inspire poetry rather than desire for possession of the beloved.

The *Julia Monobiblos* reflects as consistently on the poetics of love as on love itself. One could assume that Secundus's self-consciousness was especially strong here, as it was his first book of poetry. In the closing poem, for example, he claims that Cupid's laws and customs— in opposition to ordinary political laws or social customs—permitted the writing of such poetry. *Elegies* 1.11, moreover, consecrates the collection to the gods of love, claiming poetic success despite the demise of the affair:

> Interea hos Elegos, primi monumenta caloris,
> Accipite, et risum iungite cum gemitu,
> Dicentes: nostri pars hic quoque parva triumphi est;
> Semper amet, dulci semper amore fruens.[1]
> (*Elegies* 1.11.57–60)

[(Passage is addressed to Cupid and Venus) ... Meanwhile receive these elegies, the monuments of my first passion and join a laugh to a sigh, saying: "Herein lies, too, a small part of our triumph—may he always love, always enjoying sweet love."]

As soon as trouble arises in the "affair" (or in the amatory cycle)—first announced in *Elegies* 1.7—Secundus reflects on the idea that love is poetry. The opening lines of the poetic announcement that a rival is coming to marry Julia refers, almost nostalgically, to the poetic mission received in *Elegies* 1.1:

> Insidiose Puer, maternis saevior undis,
> Hacne tuus vates fraude petendus eram?

---

[1] MS. Rawl. G. 154, fol. 30, line 60 is a correction for the crossed out phrase "Mollia cum Domina tempore lucis habet." "Habet" was crossed out and replaced with "agat," which was also crossed out when the line was rewritten.

Tu mihi[1] iussisti, numeris levioribus irem,
Assumsi faciles ad tua iussa modos,
Materiesque mihi curvato venit ab arcu
Longa, sub undenos digna venire pedes.
Vix opus incepi; dominam, Puer improbe, tollis,
Ducis et externas in mea regna manus.
(*Elegies* 1.7.1-8)

[Treacherous boy, rougher than the waters of your mother, did
you have to defraud me, your poet? You ordered me to provide
lighter verse; I took up the facile meter, as you commanded.
Your bow brought a lengthy theme, worthy of being put in
distich. Scarcely had I begun the work—evil Boy, you are taking
away my mistress and leading foreign bands against my realm.]

Secundus has gone to war, as it were, marching to the eleven-feet
pattern of elegiac distich. Obviously in a "literary campaign," the
losses have accrued to him not only as a lover but also as a poet. In
line 24, we hear that the "delights of the poets" ("Vatum deliciis")
have been violated. Moreover, Julia could have ruled not merely him,
but him as a poet (see lines 31-34).[2] If the laws of marriage had not
interceded, he would have become a great poet:

Et poterant aliquid nostrae praestare Camenae,
Fata nisi obstarent, et male faustus[3] Hymen.
(lines 49-50)

[And my Muses could have become preeminent, were not fate
and the ill-omened Hymen against it.]

Ironically, though, after a long tribute to poets, especially amatory
poets of antiquity (lines 51-58), Secundus does claim a place for his
verses in an eternal life of literature, despite the demise of his love:

---

[1] BB, 1:43 has "quia." The reading of "mihi" in MS. Rawl. G. 154, fol. 15,
seems better.

[2] *Elegies* 1.7.31-34: "Ah, poteras, lux, ah, poteras ius dicere nobis, /
Oreque formoso regia verba loqui, / Inque meo versu sublimia regna tenere, / Prima
fidis nostrae gloria, serus honor." (Oh my light, you could have, oh, you could
have dictated law to me, spoken royal words from your beautiful mouth, ruled
over a sublime kingdom in my verse; you were the first glory of my lyre and
its last honor.)

[3] MS. Rawl. G. 154, fol. 16, "male faustus" is a correction for the crossed
out "violentus."

Nostra quoque, adveniens si non his inseret aetas.
(Quod sperare pudor sit mihi, sitque nefas)
Non tamen obscura damnabit nomina nocte.

(lines 59–61)

[Even if the future will not insert my name among these (i.e., those of ancient poets)—for which it would be shameful and sacrilegious for me to hope—nonetheless it will not damn my name to dark night.]

Literary life, at least, holds the promise of free-born Venus, as opposed to death and the silencing of poetry caused by the restrictive Hymen.

Elegies 1.10, a *Somnium* or "dream-poem," illustrates that Secundus's posture as a lover is never distinct from that as poet. In fact, his concept of "literary experience," in the context of his nugatory aesthetics, ultimately allows no sharp differentiation between the *littérateur* and lover. Obsession with the equation of love with poetry informs virtually the entirety of *Elegies* 1.10. For example, he transforms the much-used topos of the poet-lover's power (usually articulated as a menacing power) to define (and, hence, to praise or censure) the mistress into the more distinctive (and self-ironic) conceit that success with the woman is a poetic accomplishment.

Ite procul moestum, lacrimae, genus, ite querelae,
　　Et comes aligeri cura vigil Pueri.
Cinge triumphantes victrici fronde capillos
　　Laurea, Phoebeae[1] grata corona comae!
Misit in amplexus illam Venus aurea nostros,
　　Prima mihi quae fax, quae mihi serus amor.
Non fora, non portus, non iam populosa theatra,
　　Templaque sunt nostris conscia blanditiis.
Mater abest, digitis legem quae ponat et ori,
　　Et cogat tremulo murmure pauca loqui,
Osculaque aridulis non continuanda labellis
　　Carpere, quae iuret barbara, quisquis amat;
Et celare faces, et amici obtexere nomen,
　　Multaque quae solers fingere discit Amor.

---

[1] Ibid., fol. 24, "Laurea, Phoebeae" is a correction for the crossed out "Laurus Apollineae."

Sola iacet mecum semoto Iulia lecto,
  Sola tamen solos non sinit esse Venus,
Et Puer unanimes comitatus in omnia vitas,
  Certus et exanimes, certus et ossa sequi.
Forte vident et nos, qui spectant omnia, Divi,
  Deliciis nostris invidiosa cohors.
Di, precor, o nostris ne lusibus invideatis;
  Non ego nunc vestris lusibus invideo.
Iulia, te teneo; teneant sua gaudia Divi;
  Te teneo, mea lux; lux mea, te teneo.
Iulia, te teneo! Superi, teneatis Olympum.
  Quid loquor? an vere, Iulia, te teneo?
Dormio ne? an vigilo? vera haec an somnia sunt haec?
  Somnia seu, seu sunt vera,[1] fruamur age!
Somnia si sunt haec, durent haec somnia longum,
  Nec vigilem faciat me, precor, ulla dies.
Et quicumque meo pones vestigia tecto,
  Parce pedum strepitu, comprime vocis iter.
Sic tibi non umquam rumpant insomnia galli.
  Tardaque productae tempora noctis eant;
Plurima cum rubris tibi gemma legetur ab undis,
  Pactolique domus tota liquore fluet.

                                        (*Elegies* 1.10)

[Oh mournful genre, tears, go far away![2] Depart, complaints
and restless trouble, the companion of the winged boy. Oh
laurel crown, pleasing to the Apolline hair, wreathe the trium-
phant locks with your victorious fronds. Golden Venus has sent
her to my embraces, yes, she who was my first flame and who
will be my last love.[3] The forums, harbors, busy theaters and
temples do not witness our pleasure. The mother is gone—who
imposes law with gestures and word and who compels us to
speak but a little with trembling whisper and to snatch kisses

---

[1] Ibid., fol. 26, has only the reading "Somnia seu sunt, seu vera" for the
beginning of line 28.

[2] The Latin in this line has a strong echo of Pseudo-Tibullus 3.6.7: "Ite procul
durum curae genus, ite labores." This poem is by a certain "Lygdamus" whose six
elegies (Tibullus 3.1–6) celebrate a woman named Neaera.

[3] There is an echo in this line of Propertius 1.12.20: "Cynthia prima fuit,
Cynthia finis erit."

that must be short and with dry lips—kisses which every lover would decry as barbaric—and to hide the flames of love and to conceal the name of the lover (which crafty Amor teaches us to do in many ways).

Alone, Julia lies with me on a secluded bed, alone! Yet Venus alone doesn't allow us to be alone, and the boy is a companion in everything to lovers of one mind, certain to follow them as they die, certain to follow their bones. And maybe the gods, who see everything, also see us. Perhaps the group envies our delights. Gods, I pray, please don't envy our games—I don't envy yours. Julia, I hold you; may the gods hold their delights. My light, I hold you—I hold you, my light—Julia, I hold you! Gods, may you hold Olympus. What am I saying—do I truly hold you, Julia? Or am I dreaming? Or am I awake? Are these images real or are they dreams? Whether dreams or reality, come, let us enjoy them. If they are dreams, let the dreams last a long time. I pray, let the day not wake me.

If one of you comes to my door, don't walk loudly! And don't speak. Thus may the roosters never burst your dreams and may the time of the drawn-out night pass slowly, while many a jewel is gathered for you from the Red Sea and your whole house is awash in Pactolean water.[1]]

Each image and formulation, it seems, has a double valence of poetry and love. Some connections are rather obvious, such as the simultaneity of a dream of fulfillment with Julia and the attainment of the Apolline laurels, not to mention the address to the "mournful genre," a reference to the elegy and his unhappy love. The position of the mother, furthermore, defines the strictures of law and society, though there is also a hint that the erotic poet may be flouting a socio-poetic law. Indeed, that "dry kisses" ("Basia") are barbaric is a *double entendre* for kiss-poetry being unhumanistic. ("Unhumanistic" would be a primary sense of "barbarus" in the sixteenth century.) Similarly, the gods' envy of "deliciae" and "lusus" could be literary as these are terms which also mean "erotic poems," in which case Secundus is, perhaps, expressing fear that his poetry will be rejected.

---

[1] The Pactolus is a river in Lydia which was supposed to carry large quantities of gold. Secundus is thinking of Horace, *Epodes* 15.20 (a line addressed to Neaera) as well as Propertius 1.14.11.

The lover's desire for privacy also has meaning in Secundus's poetological metadiscourse. He emphasizes the lovers as being separated from the world ("semoto ... lecto"—on a removed bed). At this point in the poem, poetry is raised above the kinds of public discourse subjected to social taboos or political or religious expectations: this poetry is not known to the courts, the churches, or even the theaters (lines 7–8). And those laws which can be applied to define poetry only make it barbarous. The need to disguise love poetry has vanished in the dream as its only audience is Venus and Cupid or love itself. As we shall see, a similar desire for separation from a literary standard informs Secundus's *Basia* and *Epigrams*.

This desire for separation from criticism also has parallels in other poems from the *Julia Monobiblos*. We can read *Elegies* 1.7.85–86, the address to humankind to free Venus from the shackles of law, as an allegory of poetological liberty. Similarly, in the final poem, Secundus does not want his love to become the gossip of the town (see *Elegies* 1.11.45). In *Elegies* 1.5, he defines the only acceptable kind of judge as someone (here young men are the judges) who will experience love in the context of reading his poetry and will, therefore, admire the heat of his passion and slight words:

> At vos, qui, iuvenes, suspiria nostra notatis,
> Et fractos oculos et sine mente gradum,
> Ebria ridentes nullo cum pondere verba,
> Et si quis subito venit in ora color,
> Postmodo dicetis: non infeliciter arsit;
> Praemia quum nostri nota laboris erunt.
> (*Elegies* 1.5.93–98)

[But, young men, as you take note of my sighing, my broken eyes, my mindless gait, laughing at the drunken words without meaning, if suddenly some color flashes on your face, you shall say afterwards, when you are familiar with the rewards of my labor: "He did not burn infelicitously."[1]]

---

[1] Schoolfield, *Janus Secundus*, 81, says that "non infeliciter arsit" is "an intentional ambiguity, suggesting both 'He burned, but not in a worthless cause' and 'He did not burn in vain.'" I would add that Secundus is also making a pun on the literary sense of "infeliciter," that he did not burn in an infelicitous style.

Somnium itself is a *double entendre* meaning both the erotic dream and the erotic dream-poem. Thus the realization of the *somnium* becomes a literary achievement (or experience). The dream's status as both authentic experience and literature derives, it would seem, from Secundus's correlation of poetry and experience. As both are conflated, any question as to whether Secundus is more concerned with love than with love poetry is not only superficial but also invalid. In fact, the complexity of a reality derived from experience and imagination is poignantly conveyed in the implicit comparison of dreams: one man *dreams* of love, the other of fantastic wealth. Secundus's elegiac *Somnium* not only signifies the primacy of the subjective I, but also obviates the need to debate the status of the actual—love and love poetry are authentic experiences of Secundus's persona.

The *Elegies* taken as a whole and the *Julia Monobiblos* in particular evince many moments of poetological reflection. They thematize the discontinuity between the sincerity of the importuning lover and the disingenuity arising from the conventionality of the Renaissance elegy. *Imitatio* can be freely acknowledged, and also made the object of playfulness and irony. Moreover, the authenticity of experience is located in literature as well as life. In fact, one wonders if the distinctive vividness of Secundus's erotic poetry may not derive from a goal of forming or evoking an experience in the reader. The idea that love poetry stands apart from the larger world of politics, law, and war has several consequences. It inverts the values of society and fills the language of politics (and especially war) with new (often parodistic) meaning. As we shall see later in more detail, it also removes the poet, at least ideally, from the laws and conventions of a fixed sociopoetic standard.

Fig. 5. Secundus's Medallion of Julia (recto)
Lead; 44 mm
Reproduced courtesy of Koninklijke Bibliotheek Albert I

4 The Basia:
   Poetry and the Art of the Kiss

Quaeris, quot mihi basiationes
tuae, Lesbia, sint satis superque.
            Catullus, 7.1-2.

[You ask, Lesbia, how many of your kisses are enough and
more than enough for me.]

Tam diversa uno sic coiere choro.
            Joseph Scaliger on the *Basia*

[Thus such diverse poems have come together in a single chorus.]

The *Basia* made Secundus's reputation in the Renaissance and also
account, more than any other work, for his literary endurance in
modern times. Some experts may have read and preferred the Julia
elegies, but the *Basia* have always attracted the most interest, and
almost certainly always will. During the Renaissance, an age when
amatory poetry enjoyed perhaps its most intense vogue, authors imitated Secundus's *Basia* with an avidness exceeded, it seems, only by
their enthusiasm for Petrarch. The influence of the *Basia* was so immense and pervasive that in some cases the philologist must concede
that what appears to be an imitation of Secundus is, in fact, an imitation of an imitation.[1] Several of the greatest writers of the sixteenth
and seventeenth centuries studied and admired the *Basia*. The impact
was probably greatest in France and the Netherlands. Joachim du

---

[1] The most thorough study of the impact of the *Basia*, though it, too, is incomplete, is Ellinger's introduction to his edition of the *Basia*. See Secundus,
Basia, ed. Ellinger, x–xlv. Ellinger also considered the specific question of Secundus's impact on Goethe's *Römische Elegien* in "Goethe und Johannes Secundus."

Bellay's *Amores* has been called a "descendant of the *Basia*."[1] Pierre de Ronsard, the initiator of the *Pléiade* (the most important poetic movement in Renaissance France), cited above all the *Basia* in his hyperbolic eulogy of Secundus[2] and also translated or imitated at least ten of the *Basia*. Among other French poets to imitate the *Basia* are Labé, Bonefons, Belleau, and Baïf; in his *Essays*, Michel Montaigne counted them among his favorite books.[3] Similarly, Dutch imitators include those who wrote in Latin and the vernacular: Dousa, Lernutius, Westerbaen, Le Bleus, de Brune, and Huygens were keenly interested in Secundus and the *Basia*. There were also significant imitators among the Italians (especially Marino), the English (Sidney, Spenser, Milton, etc.), and the Germans (Weckherlin, Opitz, Fleming, Hofmannswaldau, and Günther). By the eighteenth century, Secundus's influence had become sporadic. Still, Goethe studied the *Basia* in the 1770s and wrote on 2 November 1776 his much cited poem "An den Geist des Johannes Secundus," with its memorable address "Lieber, heiliger, grosser Küsser." Also in the 1770s, none other than Mirabeau turned to Secundus during a time of duress. While imprisoned in Vincennes (1778–1780), he translated Tibullus and the *Basia* for his beloved Sophie (first published in 1796). His prose rendering has been praised for its vigor and passion, though it largely fails to convey Secundus's self-ironies.[4]

In the seventeenth century, the eminent legal scholar and *littérateur* Hugo Grotius said that, with the *Basia*, Secundus was the "inventor of a new kind of writing."[5] On the one hand, Grotius is right that Secundus invented a new kind of amatory cycle. There had never been anything quite like the *Basia* and they certainly spawned many imitators. Yet Secundus unquestionably drew his inspiration from earlier writers. Of the ancients, Catullus has pride of place as his famous poems 5 ("Vivamus mea Lesbia, atque amemus") and 7 ("Quaeris, quot mihi basiationes" . . .) are the *Basia*'s most obvious forebears. Secundus took motifs from both of them and even refers

---

[1] Endres, *Joannes Secundus*, 31.
[2] See Ronsard, *Oeuvres complètes*, ed. Laumonier, 2:422 and the epigraph to chapter two.
[3] *Basia*, ed. Ellinger, xxii.
[4] Ibid., xxxiii.
[5] Quoted by BB, 1:xxxviii.

to Catullus and Lesbia in *Basia* 16. Though not mentioned by earlier scholars, Secundus also used Catullus's homosexual kiss poems, poems 48 and 99 (both addressed to Juventus). In addition to several purloined motifs, Catullus's metrics, as well as his intensity, succinctness, and caustic wit find parallels in the *Basia*. Several kiss poems in the *Greek Anthology* also made contributions. (Secundus had known the *Greek Anthology* certainly since 1533 and perhaps since his schooldays in The Hague.) In particular, he used motifs found in Meleager, Paul the Silentiary, Pseudo-Plato, and an anonymous poem (5.305). In general, though, the Augustan poets continued to inform his style; like the *Elegies* and *Odes*, the *Basia* have reminiscences of Horace, Tibullus, Propertius, Ovid, and even Vergil.[1]

Secundus always looked to Italian humanists for models.[2] He knew Philip Beroaldus the Elder's "Panthia's Kiss" ("Osculum Panthiae"), a long tribute to his beloved, in particular to the admirable kisses she bestows. Though Beroaldus's Latin is so simple as to suggest a school exercise, he burdened his light subject with a weighty *ornatus* of classical tags. For the most part, the sheer volume of comparisons to classical figures is irritating, and, occasionally, the added distraction of an exceedingly obscure reference arises. One cannot help thinking that Secundus learned from this experience to avoid the tedium which accrues to an *accumulatio*, as it were, of classical parallels. At any rate, Secundus keeps his mythological decoration within bounds and, when he does compose a mythological poem, he enlivens it by creating a narrative. In the three mythological vignettes (*Basia* 1, 15, and 18), he focuses on compressed, entertaining narration; he never parades recondite details from classical culture in purely ekphrastic passages. Despite these differences, though, it is generally agreed that Secundus's most quoted line, "O vis superba formae" (Oh proud power of beauty), is derived from

---

[1] See Ellinger, *Geschichte der neulateinischen Literatur*, 3:66–67. Naturally, scholars have noted Secundus's dependence on ancient writers (especially Catullus, Propertius, Tibullus, Ovid, Vergil, and, as I would stress, Martial), but they are unanimous in their praise of Secundus's ability nonetheless to develop a unique style. Ellinger, for example, vouched rather flamboyantly for his uniqueness: "nichts ist äusserlich angeeignet, alles aus dem unmittelbarem Leben und der glühenden Seele des Dichters wiedergegeben worden" (p. 50).

[2] Joos, "Eenige grieksch-latijnsche en italiaansch-renaissance invloeden op de *Basia*," argues, on the basis of material derived from Burmann-Bosscha and Ellinger, that these antecedents lessen the value of Secundus's poetry.

Beroaldus's "Tantum forma valet" (Such is beauty's sway; line 33).[1]

Ellinger proposed that Secundus not only was familiar with Petrus Crinitus's kiss poem, "Ad Neaeram," but also named the beloved of the *Basia* Neaera as a bow to that work.[2] "Ad Neaeram" uses the motif of the soul being exchanged through a kiss (Crinitus's soul prefers to reside in Neaera's body); the kiss of the beloved can breathe the spirit back into the poet. Secundus unquestionably uses that motif in *Basia* 13, though there are no verbal reminiscences of "Ad Neaeram" in it. It is, of course, possible, perhaps even likely, that the similarity between the two poems is due to a common ancestry in epigram 5.78 of the *Greek Anthology* and the ancient imitation of it quoted by Aulus Gellius.[3] There is every reason to believe that the name Neaera is instead a tribute to Michele Marullo,[4] whose beloved is so-named, and to Horace, who rails against a hard hearted Neaera in *Epodes* 15. If Secundus knew Crinitus's poem, he would have admired its playfulness, but there is no indication that he found it worthy of imitation.

On the other hand, Secundus must have read Sannazaro's "Ad Ninam," a minor masterpiece of amatory poetry.[5] For one thing, Secundus seems to have imitated Sannazaro's description of kisses ("Nec quas dent bene filiae parenti / Nec quas dent bene fratribus sorores"[6] [Not those which daughters appropriately would give a parent, nor those which sisters appropriately would give their brothers]) in an account of unsatisfactory kisses that Neaera once gave: "utrumque (i.e., basium) nec longum nec udum, / Qualia teligero Diana / Det castra fratri, qualia dat patri / Experta nullos nata

----

[1] Schoolfield, *Janus Secundus*, 103, aptly characterizes the genius of Secundus's imitation of Beroaldus: "The notion may belong to Beroaldus, but the inimitable style—the outcry, the ambiguities of 'vis' and 'superba', the climax of 'forma'—is the work of Secundus." Ellinger prints Beroaldus's poem in *Basia*, 17–20.

[2] *Basia*, ed. Ellinger, vi.

[3] Both poems are printed in ibid., 20–21. See *Greek Anthology* 5.78 (an epigram by Plato), ed. and trans. Paton: "My soul was on my lips as I was kissing Agathon. Poor soul! She came hoping to cross over to him."

[4] Secundus also imitated Marullo's *Epigrams* 1.3 ("De Neaera") in *Basia* 15. See Marullus, *Carmina*, ed. Perosa, 4.

[5] The poem is also available in *An Anthology of Neo-Latin Poetry*, ed. and trans. Nichols, 310–13.

[6] *Basia*, ed. Ellinger, 22 (lines 3–4).

Cupidines" (Each kiss was neither long nor moist: they were the kind chaste Diana would give her armed brother, or the kind a girl, without experience of love, would give her father; *Basia* 9.11–14). Sannazaro's physical description of the kiss—its length, the biting and sucking of the tongue—and the listing of essences inferior to those of her kiss are recalled in Secundus's poems. Like Secundus, Sannazaro explicitly makes the kiss a *pars pro toto* for sexual intercourse as he expresses the desire that the kiss might lead to the fondling of Nina's breasts, though he decorously breaks off the description of sexual desire by listing a series of women to whom he would prefer her. Secundus, one can confidently assume, admired Sannazaro's poetic control as well as his humorous (purposefully self-ironic) lasciviousness, though Secundus, still, must be credited with a much more complex elaboration of a nugatory poetics in his *Basia*.[1]

The *Basia* are a cycle of nineteen poems that celebrate the poet's love for a Spanish woman named Neaera, presumed by scholars to have been a prostitute.[2] The poems are uniform in subject matter as all concern either kissing, or Neaera, or both; stylistic similarities include brevity, use of epigrammatic *pointe*, as well as the occurrence in each poem of an apostrophe. The variations on this limited theme—ranging from the mythological origin of the kiss, to pleas for kisses, to a rebuke for biting kisses, to an address to bees collecting honey from Neaera's lips—illustrate Secundus's ingenuity as well as elegant phraseology.[3] Another kind of variation resides in the psychology of Secundus's persona, whose moods shift from pusillanimous, to self-deprecating, to zealous and angry. The art of variation depends not only on the juxtaposition of different types of poems (such as narrative and lyrical, or those with heavy or light cadences), but also on antithesis within the poems. The quintessential *Basium* has a strong *volta* that marks a contradiction in sentiment or style. *Basia* 14, for example, moves from the reproachful "Dura / Duro marmore durior Neaera" (hard Neaera, harder than hard marble; lines 2–3) to the wheedling "Mollis / Molli mollior anseris medulla"

---

[1] Perella, *The Kiss Sacred and Profane*, 192–93, draws attention to two poems by Giovanni Pontano which Secundus may have known.

[2] See Ellinger, *Geschichte der neulateinischen Literatur*, 3:44.

[3] Secundus's ingenuity has been the principal object of admiration among critics ever since the sixteenth century; see Schoolfield, *Janus Secundus*, 101.

(soft Neaera, softer than the soft goose down; lines 12–13).[1] An additional merit of the cycle, perhaps one that is not immediately apparent to the modern reader, is Secundus's metrical virtuosity. Using eight different meters or strophic forms,[2] he shows deep sensitivity to the verve of ancient metrics, as can be seen in his light anacreontics (*Basia* 7), caustic hendecasyllabics (for example, *Basia* 12 and 14), and importuning or lugubrious pentameters (for example, *Basia* 6, 13, and 17). He even uses the pythiambic for his first mention of Neaera (*Basia* 2) to indicate one of his classical sources for her, Horace's pythiambic *Epodes* 15.[3] The astonishing element in this literary sophistication is not only that it belongs to a very young poet—Secundus was in his early twenties when he composed the *Basia*—but also that, as critics invariably note, he wears his learning lightly. Indeed, unlike the poetry of his humanist contemporaries, Secundus's *Basia* are, in translation at least, accessible to those without a classical education.

The *Basia* have always been understood as a cycle in which, though the poems can certainly be read in isolation, the whole is greater than the sum of individual parts. It is important to realize, however, that, unlike the Julia elegies, the cycle does not have a linear structure that narrates the story of an affair from beginning to conclusion. There is also no strict symmetry in the arrangement of the poems. Instead, there are some general patterns of arrangement that complement the overall structural principle of variation.

Basia 1, consciously designed as a proemium, narrates a story of the origin of the kiss.[4] It tells how, after Venus's removal of Asca-

---

[1] While the translations throughout are my own, I should note that many translations of the *Basia* are available; see, for example, the following: *An Anthology of Neo-Latin Poetry*, ed. and trans. Nichols, 486–515; *Les baisers et l'épithalame suivis des odes et des élégies*, ed. and trans. Rat; *Küsse*, trans. Wiesner; and *The Love Poems of Johannes Secundus*, ed. and trans. Wright.

[2] See discussion by Guépin, *De Kunst van Janus Secundus*, 359–76. He lists only seven meters, but is aware that *Basia* 8 and 18 are slightly different. (*Basia* 8 is iambic dimeter catalectic and *Basia* 18 is iambic trimeter catalectic.)

[3] Schroeter, *Beiträge zur Geschichte der neulateinischen Poesie*, 200, observed the important link between *Basia* 2 and *Epodes* 15.

[4] Incidentally, Guépin, *De Kunst van Janus Secundus*, 499, places *Basia* 1 before the trip to Spain. He claims that an epigram by J. C. Scaliger, which was published in 1533, mocks the mythological vignette of *Basia* 1. (See Guépin, 146–47, for the epigram.) The suggestion is interesting, but it is not by any means certain that Scaliger mocks Secundus's poem.

nius (Aeneas's son) to Mount Cythera (a setting derived from *Aeneid*
1.680ff.), she was tormented as she wanted to kiss her grandson, but
dared not disturb him in his sleep. In her frustration, she bestowed
thousands of kisses on icy rosebuds, which then, sown throughout
the earth, brought kisses to humankind.

> Cum Venus Ascanium super alta Cythera tulisset
> Sopitum teneris imposuit violis,
> Albarum nimbos circumfuditque rosarum,
> Et totum liquido sparsit odore locum.
> Mox veteres animo revocavit Adonidos ignes,
> Notus et irrepsit ima per ossa calor.
> O quoties voluit circumdare colla nepotis!
> O quoties dixit: Talis Adonis erat!
> Sed placidam pueri metuens turbare quietem
> Fixit vicinis basia mille rosis.
> Ecce calent illae, cupidaeque per ora Diones
> Aura susurranti flamine lenta subit.
> Quotque rosas tetigit tot basia nata repente
> Gaudia reddebant multiplicata Deae.
> At Cytherea natans niveis per nubila cygnis[1]
> Ingentis terrae coepit obire globum.
> Triptolemique modo fecundis oscula glebis
> Sparsit, et ignotos ter dedit ore sonos.
> Inde seges felix nata est mortalibus aegris,
> Inde medela meis unica nata malis.
> Salvete aeternum nostrae moderamina flammae,
> Humida de gelidis basia nata rosis.
> En ego sum, vestri quo vate canentur honores,
> Nota Medusaei dum iuga montis erunt,
> Et memor Aeneadum stirpisque disertus amatae,
> Mollia Romulidum verba loquetur Amor.

[When Venus had carried Ascanius to the heights of lofty
Cythera, she laid him, asleep, on soft violets and poured around
clouds of white roses and moistened the entire area with flowing
perfume. Soon she recalled the old flames of Adonis, and the fa-

---

[1] MS. Rawl. G. 154, fol. 149, "cygnis" is a correction for the crossed out
"pennis."

miliar warmth penetrated deep through her bones. Oh, how
many times did she desire to caress the neck of her grandson?
How many times did she say, "so was Adonis"? But, fearing to
disrupt the boy's sleep, she kissed nearby roses a thousand times.
Look, they grow warm and, with whispering flame, a gentle
breeze goes through the mouth of desirous Venus. As many
roses as she touched, so many kisses, suddenly born, brought
multiplied pleasures to the goddess. But, the Cytherean, flying
through the clouds on snowy swans, began to circle the globe of
the vast earth. In Triptolemus's manner, she sowed kisses on
the fertile fields and thrice made an unaccustomed sound. From
that was born a happy harvest for suffering humans. From that
was born the only cure for my malady. Greetings always, as-
suager of my flame, moist kisses born of icy roses! I am he, the
poet by whom your honors will be celebrated in song, as long
as the ridges of Mt. Medusa shall be renowned, and as long as
Amor, mindful of Aeneas's progeny and full of the eloquence of
his beloved people, shall speak the gentle words of Romulus's
descendants.]

Though obviously a proemium (and one reminiscent of an Alexandrian etiological poem), *Basia* 1 also functions by virtue of its my-
thologizing as a counterweight to the mythological poems grouped
toward the end of the cycle (*Basia* 15 and 18). As is evident in the
Vergilian *ornatus* and especially in the poetic ideal of the finale (note
the emphasis placed on "disertus" [eloquent] and the Latin language),
Secundus legitimates his poetry—despite the objections raised in subsequent *Basia*—as a humanist undertaking. The levity and inventiveness are certainly prefigurations of what is to come, but the poem's
very lightness indicates the critical edge that characterizes the poet's
persona in the *Basia*. Indeed, *Basia* 1 unmistakably mocks the high-
flying style of epic. Secundus was a master of the grandiloquent
moment, which he ironizes as a way of elevating his decidedly
unheroic, non-epic style. The introductory tone of the faux-grandilo-
quent assumes particular importance, we shall see, as it prefigures his
defense of the cultivation of the lesser art of amatory poetry. The
connection to the heroic *Aeneid* reaches its highest pitch when he
solemnly apostrophizes the kisses and vows to sing of their honors.
Whoever reads the final four lines aloud will notice the onomatopoe-
ic evocation of "soft words" ("mollia ... verba"), especially in the

liquids and nasals of the final line and the measured smoothness created, in part, by the absence of elision. The patronymic "Romulidum" indicates the heroic as does the appellation "Aeneas's progeny," with the result that the elegant formulation conveys an idea of past grandeur—the greatness that was Rome—and one that endures. But, ironically, that greatness is of the slightest and most tenuous build—as Secundus will later invocate, "I sing of kisses unarmed." He sings of erotic love, not of the arms and the man.

The proemium, thus, introduces complex tones of levity and irony as well as themes of apology and, not least, humanism, all of which recur in the cycle. The rest of the cycle may be grouped into three parts where different tonal qualities predominate. Like *Basia* 1, *Basia* 2–8 generally sound light tones, sometimes exceedingly so. The last two of that group (*Basia* 7 and 8), as glyconics and iambic dimeter catalectic, respectively, move at an almost frenzied speed, reaching a poetic climax in the last line of *Basia* 8 with "O vis superba formae." This high point of ambiguous emotion follows hard on a preliminary climax in 5.21: "Tu, tu sola mihi es, Neaera, maior" (You, you, Neaera, alone are greater to me).

The following set of poems, which holds the center of the cycle, entails considerably more graphic descriptions of sexual desire; its tone is correspondingly harsher. *Basia* 5, as a prefiguration of the center, is a sustained description of erotic kissing, whereas *Basia* 9, 10, 11, 12, and 14 either adopt or defend explicitly sexual poetics, occasionally with purposefully obscene overtones.[1] Here, the poet names the penis in both humorous and threatening formulations; he also addresses both his readers and his beloved in frank, if not coarse, terms. The final group of poems (*Basia* 15–19) is a recovery from the epigrammatic tone of the center. *Basia* 15 and 18 are light mythological narratives, *Basia* 16 a Horatian "carpe diem," *Basia* 17 an elegant "Dawn Song," though one with arresting hints of deep torment. The final poem is the most extreme example of Secundus's nugatory poetics. Critics have tended to dismiss it as silly, suggesting the poet has gotten tired.[2] I find it likely, and highly significant, that the

---

[1] Please note that these groupings are not exact. *Basia* 5 would seem to prefigure the center; *Basia* 13, though its images of exhaustion and death are metaphors for sex, does not have the rough qualities of the other poems in the center.

[2] *Basia* 19 was not included in the first publication of the cycle in 1539. Nat-

poem is an ironically self-mocking version of the slight poem cast in "mollia verba"; it comes very close to being a self-parody. It is an address to bees, urging them to move on from the usual run of elegant spices to something genuinely exquisite, namely, Neaera's lips. Especially if read from the perspective of the licentious poems of the center (and if we accept that its artificiality may be purposefully exaggerated), then it is possible to understand *Basia* 19 as a parody of the harmless amatory poem. Secundus even signals, though lightly, that the cycle is over when he concedes that he has perhaps been somewhat too "garrulous" (*Basia* 19.18: "garrulus").

Although Secundus insists that he writes for young men and women about to enjoy the pleasures of love, the *Basia* can be seen as a kind of poet's poetry, in part because they speak to literary issues such as decorum, style, and artistic freedom. Because kisses and kissing are on occasion synonymous with poems and writing poetry, one is justified in understanding "basia," on a metaphorical level, as a cipher for poetry. The title *Basia* is, of course, a *double entendre*, meaning both "kisses" and "kiss-poems." Secundus exploits this double sense in several poems. In *Basia* 8, for example, the tongue is described as the organ of both kissing and poeticizing. In vivid language, Secundus asserts that, though wounded in the dangerous activity of "kissing," his tongue will never stop creating "basia" for Neaera. In a programmatic poem (*Basia* 10), he describes an aesthetic of kissing with language clearly intended to define the style of his literary *Basia*:

> Diversis varium ludat uterque modis.
> At quem deficiet varianda figura priorem,
>   Legem submissis audiat hanc oculis:
> Ut, quot utrinque prius data sint, tot basia solus
>   Dulcia victori det, totidemque modis.
>
> (lines 18–22)

[Each one should play with variation, using different styles. Whoever, as the first, cannot vary the form, should hear this rule with downcast eyes: as many kisses as were given before on

---

urally, it is impossible to know what changes or deletions Secundus might have made, had he lived to see the *Basia* through press. See Schoolfield, *Janus Secundus*, 116, on the supposed weaknesses of the poem.

both sides, so many sweet kisses must he alone give the winner, and in as many different styles.]

Such a strong verbal association between kisses and poems about kisses should make us suspect that the *Basia* concern more than just the longings of a poet in love.

In two central poems (*Basia* 11 and 12), Secundus defends his *Basia* against criticism. Though the erotic element of kissing is the literal subject of *Basia* 11, the literary sense of poetry is strongly implied.

> Basia lauta nimis quidam me iungere dicunt,
> > Qualia rugosi non didicere patres.
> Ergo, ego cum cupidis stringo tua colla lacertis,
> > Lux mea, basiolis immoriorque tuis,
> Anxius exquiram quid de me quisque loquatur?
> > Ipse quis, aut ubi sim, vix meminisse vacat.[1]
> Audiit et risit formosa Neaera, meumque
> > Hinc collum nivea cinxit et inde manu;
> Basiolumque dedit, quo non lascivius umquam
> > Inseruit Marti Cypria blanda suo;
> Et, quid, ait, metuis turbae decreta severae?
> > Causa meo tantum competit ista foro.

[Some say I give kisses that are too refined, not the kind that our wrinkled fathers learned. Therefore, when I embrace your neck with desirous arms, my light, and when I die for your little kisses, should I anxiously ask what someone might say about me? Scarcely can I still remember who or where I am. Beautiful Neaera heard and laughed; here and there she embraced my neck with her snowy hand and she bestowed a little kiss, no less sexy than any that sweet Venus fixed on her Mars. And she said: "Why do you fear the decision of the moralistic crowd? Only my court has competence in that case."]

According to him, his critics fault the "basia" as being "too refined" (line 1) and "unlike those our wrinkled fathers learned" (line 2). The point is, of course, that, while refinement and artistry remain a part of his aesthetic, Secundus emphatically rejects the need for con-

---

[1] MS. Rawl. G. 154, fol. 162, "vix meminisse vacat" is an emendation of the crossed out "non meminisse libet."

formity to a style. The sense of the "rugosi patres" (wrinkled fathers) further implies that a concept of literary didacticism or moralizing is being rejected. The poem, in fact, uses the topos of the confused lover not only to express the depth of the lover's infatuation but also to reveal the poet's disorientation from any socioliterary standard (see especially line 6). The poem concludes, presumably in the poet's imagination, with Neaera's assertion that only her judgment of "kisses" matters (lines 11–12). The metaphor of Neaera's forum or court ("meo foro") is a device that excludes any larger, perhaps official, public from determining poetry's style or judging its value. Secundus achieves, at least ideally, artistic license by inscribing the standard for its criticism into the poetry itself. For example, Neaera is able to judge his poetry with explicit commentary, as is the case here, or, as elsewhere, in the form of a gesture. She is, moreover, not his only judge.

Secundus can be much franker in laying a claim to artistic freedom. In *Basia* 12, he imitates the hendecasyllabic invective of Catullus and Martial to discredit, if not offend, his detractors:

> Quid vultus removetis hinc pudicos,
> Matronaeque puellulaeque castae?
> Non hic furta Deum iocosa canto
> Monstrosasve libidinum figuras;
> Nulla hic carmina mentulata, nulla,
> Quae non discipulos ad integellos
> Hirsutus legat in schola magister.
> Inermes cano basiationes,
> Castus Aonii chori sacerdos.
> Sed vultus adhibent modo huc protervos
> Matronaeque puellulaeque cunctae,
> Ignari quia forte mentulatum
> Verbum diximus, evolante voce.
> Ite hinc, ite procul, molesta turba,
> Matronaeque puellulaeque turpes.
> Quanto castior est Neaera nostra,
> Quae certe sine mentula libellum
> Mavult, quam sine mentula poetam.

[Why do you turn away your modest faces, chaste women and little girls? I do not sing herein of the naughty trysts of the gods, or horrifying examples of lusts—no poems with penises here; nothing that a shaggy teacher couldn't read in school to his wholesome schoolboys. I, as a chaste priest of the Aonian chorus, sing of kisses unarmed. But now all the women and little girls are turning their impudent faces toward me because, in my hasty talk, I've accidentally said the word penis. Away, far away, you molesting crowd, you women and little girls! How much more chaste is my Neaera, who certainly prefers a book without a penis to a poet without one.]

The poem divides neatly into two equal parts: the facetious address to "chaste" woman and girls (lines 1–9); and a sharp rebuke of their lewdness (lines 10–18). The first line is parodied at the *volta*: the faces of modesty ("vultus ... pudicos") become those of shamelessness ("vultus ... protervos"). His protestations of innocence are mockingly lighthearted and also engage a disarmingly direct crudity. Secundus's humorous flippancy becomes transparent in the mock heroic formulation of his undertaking: "I sing of kisses unarmed" (line 8). Using the device of the *preteritio*, he lists the offensive elements he claims to forgo in his poetry. The purpose of the list, which refers with increasing vividness to sex, is to offend his audience in the act of protesting that his poetry is inoffensive; to paraphrase Secundus, his poetry contains no intrigues of gods, no monstrous figures of lust, and no poems with penises (lines 3–5). The subsequent assertion that the business of "mentulatum" (a crude term for "having a penis") just slipped out would, in any event, be specious and, in light of the poem's virtually mathematical organization, is all the more comical.

Even the sharp invective combines the caustic with the humorous. Beginning with the abrupt correction of the epithet "castae," he inveighs against the women who, he alleges, are keenly interested in his racy language. The transparent misrepresentation of the reason for the women's interest alleviates to a degree the sharpness of his reproach. Nonetheless, the ensuing invective, stylistically reminiscent of Catullus and Martial, brands the women a "molesta turba" (molesting crowd; line 14). The *coup de grace* is a piece of twisted logic: Neaera is "purer" than the ladies because they are obsessed with poems with penises while she prefers a poet with one. In this case, the invective and obscenity both defend and demonstrate his freedom from a moralistic concept of poetry. Nonetheless, humor undercuts the crudity in two ways. His poem is an ironic protestation of innocence that admits and proves guilt. And the unconcerned repetition of "mentula" and "mentulatum" gives the poem a tone of harmlessness. After all, he sings but of "inermis basiationes" (unarmed kisses; line 8). Moreover, *Basia* 12 depends heavily on Martial, 3.68, which (together with 3.69) deals with the literary use of obscenity. Epigram 3.68, addressed to Martial's "matrona" (*Basia* 12 is similarly addressed to "matronae"), apologizes for the obscenity that will follow in the concluding poems of Book Three. Martial initially warns her that he will henceforth name the symbol of Priapus (i.e., the erect phallus) in unambiguous terms. In the denouement (which obviously inspired Secundus's portrayal of the "matronaeque puellulaeque" in *Basia* 12), Martial asserts that now the "matrona" will actually read his remaining poems with greater interest.[1]

While Secundus, as is apparent in the *Basia* (and two complementary epigrams[2]), uses irony, obscenity and invective in order to resist the potential impingements of a moralistic literary code, it is also important not to overlook his use of violence as a transgressive device. In fact, several poems describe the erotic as a longing for violence. *Basia* 8, one of the best known in the cycle because of its "O vis superba formae," recounts Neaera's ferocity, in particular her cannibalistic abuse of the poet's tongue. More common, however, are the poet's threats of violence. In *Basia* 7, he speaks, using Ovidian military metaphor, of conquering his love in "an unrelenting assault" ("ferrem continuo impetu"; line 10). Elsewhere he vows to kiss

---

[1] See Martial 3.68.7-12:

Schemate nec dubio, sed aperte nominat illam,
Quam recipit sexto mense superba Venus,
Custodem medio statuit quam vilicus horto,
Opposita spectat quam proba virgo manu.
Si bene te novi, longum iam lassa libellum
Ponebas, totum nunc studiosa leges.

[Without recourse to an ambiguous trope, (Terpsicore) now openly names that which haughty Venus receives in the sixth month and that which an overseer sets up as a guard in the middle of the garden (i.e., statue of Priapus), which an honest maiden looks at with her hands blocking it. Unless I'm wrong about you, you have been putting my long book aside in your boredom, but now, eagerly, you're reading all of it.]

[2] See *Epigrams* 1.24 and 1.58 as well as the discussion of them in chapter five.

Neaera so roughly that her body will be covered with bruises (*Basia* 10.5-9). This image is even more brutal because in *Basia* 10, as elsewhere, we must understand kissing as a synecdoche for sexual intercourse.

Basia 14, a sophisticated, though provocatively ambiguous, poem, is a frank admission by Secundus that he is not so much interested in kissing as in having sex. Ever seeking to violate a code of decorum, he expresses this desire in a crude, albeit characteristically vivid image:

> Quid profers mihi flammeum labellum?
> Non te, non volo basiare, dura,
> Duro marmore durior, Neaera.
> Tanti istas ego ut osculationes
> Imbelles faciam, superba, vestras,
> Ut, nervo toties rigens supino,
> Pertundam tunicas meas, tuasque,
> Et, desiderio furens inani,
> Tabescam miser, aestuante vena?
> Quo fugis? remane, nec hos ocellos,
> Nec nega mihi flammeum labellum:
> Te iam, te volo basiare, mollis,
> molli mollior anseris medulla.

[Why do you offer me your flame-red little lips? I do not wish to kiss you, hard Neaera, harder than hard marble. So that I would render those unwarlike kisses of yours, arrogant woman, of such value that so many times stiff, with my penis erect, I would pierce my tunic and yours and raging with mindless desire I, an unfortunate, would shrivel with my penis seething? Where are you fleeing? Stay! Don't deny me those little eyes, those flame-red lips! You, now, you I desire to kiss, soft girl, softer than the soft goose down.[1]]

The description of the erect penis attempting to penetrate clothing (lines 6-7), as Bosscha and Burmann noted, is taken from Catullus

---

[1] It would be possible, I should point out, to construe "mollis" as nominative (and therefore a reference to the poet) instead of vocative (making it, as I render it, a reference to Neaera).

32.[1] Secundus, however, imitates Catullus neither to conform to a convention of ancient eroticism nor to excuse his crudity on the grounds, say, that he has merely imitated an ancient poet. We can be confident that the image is meant to be repellent because Secundus describes Neaera's reaction to it: she flees. Her rejection of the poet's crudity is yet another instance of an audience being shocked by his poetry. The denouement in this case is a brilliant rebuff to such an audience. Although his poem's vulgarity has already transgressed the literary code, Secundus feigns conformity to convention in his finale by retracting his demand for sex instead of mere kisses. The retraction in lines 11–13, a parody of lines 1–3, would seem to embody the consummate expression of gentle, harmless eroticism. By now, however, it is clear what "te volo basiare" (line 12) means. Secundus, of course, does not really accede to his audience's expectations for less crude poetry. He ironizes the audience's expectation by parodying a gentler form of eroticism. Read from this perspective, the conclusion is a parodistic euphemism that mocks the audience's (i.e., Neaera's) reaction to his graphic description of sexual lust.

Basia 9 also invokes the image of Neaera in flight, though here the reason for her escape is much more disturbing.[2] Despite the final assertion that the poem is about a harmless punishment of kisses, *Basia* 9 suggests rape. In it, Secundus narrates a desire that, though pathological, has classical antecedents. Paul the Silentiary, whose epigrams Secundus had studied, describes his rape of Menecratis.[3] Above all, however, Secundus imitates the occasionally violent style of Ovid.[4] Ovid, for example, speaks of beating Corinna, his mistress, in several poems (*Amores* 1.7 and 2.5, for example) and, moreover, describes a scene in which he forces himself on her, after having ripped off her clothing (*Amores* 1.5). In the poet's recounting, Corinna resists his intrusion, but does so disingenuously and badly. According to Ovid, she really wants to lose the struggle:

---

[1] See BB, 1:277.

[2] A third depiction of Neaera in flight is *Basia* 3, though the image is not well developed.

[3] See *Greek Anthology* 5.275.

[4] Ovid is, of course, known for the militaristic metaphors in his erotic poems, one his most famous lines being the already quoted "Militat omnis amans" (*Amores* 1.9.1).

Pugnabat tunica sed tamen illa tegi.
Quae cum ita pugnaret, tamquam quae vincere nollet,
Victa est non aegre proditione sua.

(Amores 1.5.14–16)

[But she fought to put her clothes back on. Yet she fought as
one who did not want to win. She was conquered, quite nicely,
by her own betrayal.]

Secundus's story runs as follows: Neaera cheats him of some
kisses; he chases and eventually overpowers her; he then forces kisses
on her. Rape does not literally occur, but the account of the imag-
ined chase includes violent constrainment of Neaera:

> Et te remotis in penetralibus,
> Et te latebris abdito in intimis:[1]
>   Sequar latebras usque in imas,
>   In penetrale sequar repostum:
> Praedamque victor fervidus in meam
> Utrimque heriles iniiciens manus,
>   Raptabo, ut imbellem columbam
>   Unguibus accipiter recurvis.
> Tu deprecantes victa dabis manus,
> Haerensque totis pendula brachiis,
>   Placare me septem iocosis
>   Basiolis cupies inepta.
> Errabis.

(Basia 9.17–29)

[Hide in the farthest chamber and in the most remote hiding-
place. I will follow you all the way into the deepest hiding
place; I will follow into the most remote chamber, and, as a
burning victor over my quarry, I will drag you off, laying both
mastering hands on you, just as the hawk carries off the unwarlike dove in its crooked talons. Conquered, you will give me
your imploring hands, and clinging, as you hang on, with both
arms, you will try to placate me—oh you fool—with seven playful kisses. You will fail!]

---

[1] MS. Rawl. G. 154, fol. 160, "abdito in intimis" is an emendation of the
crossed out "abde sub intimis."

Rape is suggested in the passage's language: the flight and pursuit suggest intercourse ("in penetrale ... repostum"); the attacker emphasizes his lust and violence ("fervidus victor" ... "heriles iniciens manus"); and Neaera is described as a defenseless victim ("praedam" ... "victa"). It is also possible to associate the simile of the hawk catching the innocent dove in its hooked talons, by itself a stark image of brutality, with rape. Though other sources cannot be ruled out,[1] the simile is probably taken from Ovid's account of Arethusa's flight from Alpheus, when he attempted to rape her:

> Sic ego currebam, sic me ferus ille premebat,
> Ut fugere accipitrem penna trepidante columbae,
> Ut solet accipiter trepidas urgere columbas.[2]
>
> (*Metamorphoses* 5.604–6)

[Thus I was fleeing and thus that beast was in hot pursuit; I, just as doves, on quivering wing, are wont to flee the hawk; and he, just as the hawk chases the quivering doves.]

Furthermore, the verb "raptare," while it has the primary sense of "to seize and carry off," also means "to seize in order to rape."[3] Even the conclusion, despite its pose of innocuity, remains disturbing: Neaera will have to give the poet seven times the number of unreturned kisses, and, furthermore, she will be happy in the future to endure such punishment as he metes out.[4] Thus, for several reasons, not the least of which is that "basium" also signifies sexual intercourse, the conclusion retains a dark irony.

This poem, in effect, can be read as a metaphor of transgressive poetics. Secundus orders Neaera to flee from him, just as he seeks to put off his audience. His threat of sexual violation corresponds to his

---

[1] Secundus probably also knew Pontano's "Ad Stellam" (*Eridanus* 1.9), which also portrays a violent encounter between lovers, though one whose violence is both more reciprocal and, perhaps, more sensual than Secundus's. Guépin prints the poem in *De Kunst van Janus Secundus*, 156–59.

[2] Horace also used this simile to describe Caesar's pursuit of Cleopatra in *Odes* 1.37.17–18. The phrase "imbelles columbae" is taken from Horace, *Odes* 4.4.31–32: "neque imbellem feroces / progenerant aquilae columbae."

[3] See the *Oxford Latin Dictionary*, 1574, under "rapto."

[4] *Basia* 9.34–36: "Iurabis omnes per Veneres tuas / Te saepius poenas easdem / Crimine velle pari subire" (You will swear by all your Veneres that you often wish to endure the same punishment for the same crime).

threatened violation of the sensibilities of a prudish audience. The denouement represents, of course, the Secundian posture that his poetry is, in actuality, harmless. The violence in both language and sexual desire may result, as a consequence of the layers of irony, in a successful demonstration of poetic license, but, as a result of flouting a moralistic or decorous literary code, it also inscribes—perhaps carelessly or unwittingly—a misogynist ideology into his poetry.

In the *Basia*, Secundus's transgressive poetics has several important elements and consequences. He frequently inserts an audience into his poems in order to create tension between his licensed style and a moralistic system of literary decorum. In fact, the audience exists in such varied forms as the "matronaeque puellulaeque" (*Basia* 12), an indefinite "quidam" (*Basia* 11), and Neaera herself (especially *Basia* 11 and 14). Moreover, he does not pretend to break the literary conventions of ancient eroticism, but rather a socioliterary code he postulates for his own time. His principal devices of transgression are obscenity, invective, and, above all, vivid portrayals of sexual desire. Secundus not only seeks to shock, he also increases the violent element in his eroticism to the point of threatening to rape Neaera. He offends in order to validate his poetics, but in the process of opposing an ideological concept of poetry he articulates a licensed code that includes portraying or threatening violence against women. Of course, this is not to say that his self-irony and levity cannot also work to qualify his transgressive gestures. However, despite Secundus's ironic levity, it is important not to overlook the implications of *Basia* 9, both as an illustration of literary transgression and the limitlessness of his license.

Consequently, the *Basia* illustrate that a principal element of Secundus's poetics is the tension between his conformity to literary convention and his contravention of decorum. His poems embody a basic contradictoriness: they are derivative yet deeply original; they are charming and importuning but also offensive and repelling; their language is, at different times, both elegantly refined and brashly obscene. Over all, the *Basia* negotiate conformity to, and defiance of, assumed literary codes.

5   *The* Epigrams:
Love, Art, and License

Adeste, hendecasyllabi, quot estis
Omnesque undique, quotquot estis omnes.
    Catullus 42.1–2

[Come here, you epigrams, all of you from everywhere, the entire
number of you.]

Haec urant pueros, haec urant scripta puellas.
    Propertius 3.9.45

[May these poems set boys and girls on fire.]

Secundus's brothers collected and organized the extant epigrams in
two books. With a few restorations by the later editor Petrus
Scriverius, the first book now consists of seventy-six original compositions, while the second book comprises a collection of seventeen
Latin renderings of epigrams from the *Greek Anthology*.[1] As one
would expect, the original epigrams of Book One exhibit stylistic and
thematic diversity. The ancient models are Catullus, Martial, the
Greek Anthology, and Ausonius; of the moderns, Marullo exerted the
greatest influence. Subjects range from imitations of Catullan spar-
row-poems,[2] tributes to love and lovers,[3] encomiastic tributes to
Charles V,[4] and panegyrics on writers such as Marullo and Alciati,[5]

---

[1] Nicolaus Grudius and Hadrianus Marius did not include what are now, following Burmann and Bosscha's numeration, 1.25, 1.26, and 1.58 in their edition of
1541; these poems were, however, printed in Petrus Scriverius's edition of 1631.

[2] *Epigrams* 1.7 and 1.8.

[3] *Epigrams* 1.3, 1.4, 1.16, 1.20, 1.52, 1.53, 1.55, 1.56, and 1.57.

[4] *Epigrams* 1.17 and 1.20.

[5] *Epigrams* 1.32 and 1.33 are tributes to Marullo; 1.23 and 1.59 are accolades
of Alciati,

to lampoons on undesirable women,[1] unusual sexual behavior,[2] and prostitutes ill-disposed to the poet.[3] The tone, thus, shifts frequently between encomiastic and invective. Of all of Secundus's poetic books, the *Epigrams* offer the most sustained commentary on art,[4] and, like the *Basia*, they exemplify and espouse a concept of literature unfettered by moralistic poetics. To a degree, the defense of license engages the classical tradition, especially in the form of imitation of polemically self-apologetic works by Catullus and Martial. But all is not imitation, for in many poems Secundus reflects deeply and independently on the nature of poetry and its relationship to socio-political expectations.

In his elegies, odes, and especially in the *Basia*, Secundus's style is often epigrammatic. Some of the *Basia*, though obviously not those written in lyric meters, could have been included in the collection of epigrams. Several of them use an antithetical structure, are written in epigrammatic meters (especially the hendecasyllabics and the elegiac couplets), and reach an epigrammatic *pointe*. *Basia* 3, in fact, embodies the Catullan style of an erotic epigram:

> Da mihi suaviolum, dicebam, blanda puella:
>   Libasti labris mox mea labra tuis.
> Inde, velut presso qui territus angue resultat,
>   Ora repente meo vellis ab ore procul.
> Non hoc suaviolum dare, lux mea, sed dare tantum
>   Est desiderium flebile suavioli.[5]

[I was saying, "sweet girl, give me a little kiss"; soon you grazed my lips with yours. Thereupon, like someone who jumps back, terrified after stepping on a snake, you suddenly tear your mouth away from mine. My dear, that is not a little kiss, but rather just the tearful longing for a little kiss.]

---

[1] See *Epigrams* 1.5 and 1.76.

[2] See *Epigrams* 1.10, 1.70, and 1.72.

[3] See *Epigrams* 1.11, 1.12, 1.13, 1.22 (to Neaera), 1.29, 1.34, and 1.35.

[4] Literature is the most prominent art, though several poems deal with paintings (*Epigrams* 1.39 [on Jan van Scorel], 1.42, and 1.71), medallions or sculpture (1.43 and 1.44), and architecture (1.45).

[5] See Guépin, *De Kunst van Janus Secundus*, 28–29, for a parallel to *Basia* 3, Pontano's "Ad Cinnamam blande" (*Partenopaeus* 1.24).

Unlike much of his other poetry, however, the epigrams, as a collection, tend not to focus on love as passion. Instead, they have a harder, frequently insensitive, edge. In fact, most of the erotic epigrams offer a crude, often abusive, commentary on sex or on women (and, to a lesser degree, men[1]) as sex objects; they are usually humorous at the woman's expense.

One exception to this is *Epigrams* 1.22,[2] a poem addressed to Neaera that, as is so often the case in Roman love poetry, portrays the riven *persona* of a tormented male lover torn between love and revilement of a woman:

> Lumina mi atque animum cepit tua candida forma;
>   Moribus offendor, torva Neaera, tuis.
> Nec mihi nuda places, sed cum vestita recumbis:
>   Basia me capiunt; non amo concubitus.
> Quot dotes natura dedit, totidem tibi mendas
>   Addidit, et tamen, heu, tete ego depereo.
> Nimirum coecus non est cum pulcra tuetur;
>   Tunc Argum, tunc et Lyncea vincit Amor.
> At mendas spectare aversa fronte recusat,
>   Tunc et Tiresia coecior et Thamyra.

[Your bright beauty captured my eyes and soul; but, dreadful Neaera, your behavior offends me. You do not please me when you are nude, but rather when you recline with your clothes on. Your kisses captivate me—I do not desire sex. For every gift, nature also gave you a flaw, but, alas, I nevertheless love you desperately. Certainly, a man is not blind when he sees beauty—Amor conquers both Argus and Lynceus. But, then, blinder than Tiresias and Thamyras, he refuses to see the flaws before his eyes.]

This poem illustrates the typical Secundian antithesis, which, in addition to irony, is perhaps the most common device in the epigrams. Contrasts inform every thought of the poem: Neaera's beauty and depravity (lines 1–2); the poet's innocence and Neaera's hard-core sexuality (lines 3–4); nature's gifts and flaws (lines 5–6); beauty's power over those with keen vision (Argus and Lynceus; lines 7–8)

---

[1] See *Epigrams* 1.2 and 1.27.
[2] The only other exception is *Epigrams* 1.52.

and love's ability to make them blind (Tiresias and Thamyras; lines 9–10). Secundus adopts a Catullan *persona* of the young man who, in his supposed innocence, passionately loves a woman, even though he sees her terrible flaws all too clearly—Catullus's "Odi et amo" (I hate and I love; Catullus 85), for example, comes to mind immediately. Moreover, Secundus connects the individual struggle, aphoristically, to the general observation that humankind remains vulnerable to emotion, despite its faculty for dispassionate judgment. The almost algebraic order of the poem suggests rational control (and the potentially salutary force of disillusion), but the controlled structure intensifies the awful sense of agony that arises from embracing—consciously, but irrationally—an illusory desire.

Like Catullus and Martial (and in ways reminiscent of Juvenal's satires), Secundus also wrote political epigrams. The presence of political poems in his oeuvre raises questions about the consistency and meaningfulness of his allegiance to an amatory poetics that aggressively resists the encroachments of political subject matters. These issues are so important that I suspend thorough discussion of them until chapter six. Nonetheless, I should stress that political poems, all of which are connected in some way to Charles V or his court, figure prominently in Secundus's *Epigrams*.

Two epigrams written to accompany Nicolaas Hogenberg's *De Triomftocht van Karel V* (a series of forty engravings commemorating Charles V's coronation at Bologna in 1530), acknowledge the place of political art and also, as one would expect, sing the praises of Charles V. *Epigrams* 1.43 invites one to view the depictions of imperial and papal power and also comments on the legitimacy of political art, in clichéed fashion, as the means of attaining immortality, or at least an enduring memorial—art ensures the eternal life, as it were, of the arms and the man, though history's hero must support the arts for the sake of his own survival. As we shall see, the movement from political subject to reflection on the nature of art (or an artwork) recurs in Secundus's poems on political figures. Moreover, he creates an *aprosdochesis* with an abrupt apostrophe in the *pointe* to "posteritas vivida" (oh living posterity; line 6), claiming that art is for posterity and implying that it does not serve Charles exclusively.

Epigrams 1.44 is a more emphatic tribute to Charles, though it, too, celebrates the endurance of art in contrast to the transitoriness of a ruler's life:

> Caesar et Hesperiis, et qui dominaris Eois,
>   Accipe, quod tenebris te prohibebit opus.
> Non fato veniente cades, multosque secutus,
>   Ignotum longa nocte premere caput:
> Sed cum victuris victurus, Carole, chartis
>   Ibis ad Antipodum regna, secutus avum.

[Emperor, lord over West and East, accept this work which will save you from the shades of death! When death comes, you shall not fall; nor will your head, following the many, be pressed into oblivion by the lengthy night. Rather, Charles, you shall endure with these enduring pages and shall go to the realms on the other side, following your grandfather.]

Once again, the Secundian epigram has a binary style, though here the pairs are both geminations and antitheses. Thus we have both east and west; both Charles and the engravings will endure (line 5: "cum victuris victurus, Carole, chartis"); and the repetition of "secutus" (lines 3 and 6) sets Charles apart from the many.[1] Obviously, Secundus manipulates the myth of Charles's empire, the realm upon which the sun never sets (because of the territories in the new world, "the realms on the other side"). He uses this absence of night from the Hapsburg empire for the conceit that art *and* the realm will spare Charles the "longa nox" of death (line 4). The *pointe*, thus, includes an ingenious bow to the dynasty in the words "secutus avum" (which designates Maximilian I) and also uses the concept of the antipodal people (i.e., those on the other side of the earth[2]) to refer both to the empire in the Americas and to Hapsburg transcendence of mortality, or "this world."

Of the Caroline epigrams, there remain two witty tributes to the emperor (*Epigrams* 1.17 and 1.21) as well as two sharp invectives against Charles's enemy Francis I (*Epigrams* 1.25 and 1.26). I shall discuss *Epigrams* 1.17 and the poems against Francis in chapter six; for now, however, it is important to consider the casual style Secundus adopts in his epigrams, even when they concern Charles V. *Epigrams*

---

[1] There seems to be an imperial Roman sense of deification at work here, though that idea is expressed most clearly in *Epigrams* 1.17.

[2] Secundus may actually be thinking of Pliny's description of the Hyperboreans in *Naturalis Historia* 4.80.

1.21 may even ironize the panegyric elevation of its subject, though, at the very least, it illustrates Secundus's tendency to lower the stylistic level of political panegyric to approximate the levity of his nugatory aesthetic. Obviously, *Epigrams* 1.21 is a minor, occasional poem, written as a joke to explain the bad weather for Charles's birthday on 24 February 1531.

> Cur nive Caesareus gelida natalis inhorret?
> Candida uti foret haec lux, voluere Dei.
> Cur igitur Phoebus latet aureus? haud opus illo est:
> Phoebeum fundit Caesar ab ore iubar.
>
> (*Epigrams* 1.21) .

[Why does Caesar's birthday bristle with gelid snow? The Gods wanted the light of this day to be bright. Why, then, is golden Apollo invisible? There's no need of him: the emperor emits Apolline radiance from his countenance.]

The exaggerated tribute in the *pointe* comes close to parodying encomiastic art. Even if the poem is not critically self-parodistic, its impressive lightness and humorous tone make the tribute unusual: the hyperbolic conceit gives the epigram an intentional weightlessness that, to a degree, belies the imperial dignity of its subject.

Overshadowing politics, art emerges as a dominant theme in the epigrams. In many of his works—and with particular emphasis in the *Epigrams*—the experience of art becomes the salient feature in the stylization of his life. Obviously, the idea of experiencing love informs his poetics; but much more important is the observation that amatory poetry is itself an experience of erotic *art*, not just (or not even necessarily) an experience of real love. The underlying idea of Secundus's imitative aesthetic—i.e., art informs both experience and subsequent art—comes to the fore as a discrete theme in several of his epigrams.[1] Art is, perhaps, the single most common subject in the

---

[1] See, for example, *Epigrams* 1.20, which is an amatory tribute to Propertius's lover Cynthia. An idea of experiencing passion through art also occurs in *Epigrams* 1.66 (to Cranefeldius). Secundus even senses the perfume in Resende's poetry, according to *Epigrams* 1.67. See also the tributes to Marullo's poetry as a source of erotic verse (*Epigrams* 1.32 and 1.33). Martyn, "The Relationship between Lúcio Ângelo André de Resende and Iohannes Secundus," offers a translation of *Epigrams* 1.67, 1.74, and 1.75 (all addressed to Resende) as well as some biographical notes.

Epigrams: many are inscriptions for works of art (1.4, 1.5, 1.16, 1.42, 1.43, 1.44, and 1.47); many comment on fellow poets or artists (1.18, 1.30, 1.31, 1.32, 1.33, 1.40, 1.41, 1.65, 1.66, 1.67, 1.74, and 1.75); and several comment on, or defend, his own poetry (1.18, 1.24, 1.38, 1.47, 1.58, 1.73).

In his addresses to fellow poets (and to scholars for that matter), Secundus usually does not indulge in the stilted praise so endemic to later humanist Latin poetry.[1] He consistently executes his laudations in a casual style, frequently ironizing encomium—albeit lightly—with humorous conceits. For instance, a poetic tribute to Joannes Brassicanus, which complements the gift of a portrait medallion, issues a challenge to the young poet to write more poetry:

> Sculpsi, quodque manus et caela dedere peregi,
> Exanimum spectas et sine voce caput.
> Utque diu vivas per nos in imagine parva,
> Longaque conspicias secula, mutus eris.
> Ergo age, perpetuum lapidi tu, Iane, silenti
> Carmine vocali, si potes, adde sonum.

(Epigrams 1.65)

[I sculpted and completed all that hands and chisels could, and you see a soulless head without a voice. As long as, through my effort, you live on in this small portrait and observe the long centuries, you will be mute. Therefore, Joannes, if you can, with tuneful song add perpetual voice to the silent stone.]

Several poems critique the artistry of other poets, usually, though not always, by applying stylistic criteria of erotic verse.[2] *Epigrams* 1.31, for instance, valorizes the amatory elegy over heroic verses:

> Dum tu elegos dicis quae heroica carmina scribis,
> Dignus eras veros qui faceres elegos.

---

[1] See Erich Trunz, "Der deutsche Späthumanismus," 147–81.

[2] Two critical poems which do not refer to amatory style, though, are the lampoons of a certain Bubalus (1.40 and 1.41). *Epigram* 1.41 concerns the poet writing about his own illnesses, a fairly common theme for humanist love-poets. In a clever but crude conceit, the diseased body becomes the source of bad poetry: "Bubalus aegrotat: Paean, succurre poetae, / Ne, quotiens languet, tam mala verba vomat" (Bubalus is sick! Paean [or Apollo], heal the poet lest as often as he languishes he vomit sick words).

[While you called the heroic poems you write elegies, you were
worthy of writing real elegies.]

Consequently, it is not by accident that, in the literary-critical epigrams, Secundus accords the highest praise to Marullo, the premier,
albeit controversial, amatory poet of the preceding generation.[1]
According to *Epigrams* 1.32 (addressed to the Mechlin schoolmaster
Franciscus Hoverius), Marullo is an inexhaustible treasury for poets,
though it is his nugatory poetics—described in Catullan terminology—that gives his work literary value.

> En, Francisce, redit tuus Marullus,
> Aeque cultus ut ante, dives aeque,
> Nec vel versiculo minutus uno:
> Thesaurum tamen ille iam reliquit
> Nobis ex opibus suis perennem,
> Nullo pauperior nec asse factus.
> Qua pro re domino tot esse grates
> Relatas cupimus, quot expolitos
> Versus continet optimus Marullus,
> Quot sales lepidos, iocosque molles,
> Quot laudes veterum pias Deorum.

>   (*Epigrams* 1.32)

[Look, Franciscus, your Marullo returns to you, just as elegant
and just as rich as before. He has not been diminished by so
much as a single little verse; he nonetheless has left an inexhaustible treasury of his wealth with me, though he has not
been made even a penny poorer. For this, I desire to convey
thanks to you, dear headmaster, to the same extent to which
wonderful Marullo contains polished verses, charming jests,
gentle trifles and pious hymns to the ancient gods.[2]]

Secundus strives for the entertaining conceit (here the idea of taking
from the book without diminishing its contents) and elegant phraseology—note the chiastic *ploche* (i.e., duplication) "aeque cultus ...

---

[1] For a biography of Marullo, see Kidwell, *Marullus*, though Kidwell is unaware of Marullo's impact on Secundus.

[2] Secundus refers here to Marullo's *Hymni naturales* which raised considerable controversy in the Renaissance, especially from Poliziano, for their alleged
paganism.

dives aeque," the parallelism of "minutus" and "factus" as well as
the graceful anaphora of "quot ... quot ... quot." Most important,
though, is his use of a Catullan standard of nugatory poetics to inform the praise of the "expolitos / versus," "sales lepidos," and
"iocosque molles." *Epigrams* 1.33 reiterates the classical standard for
amatory style, including this time both Catullus[1] and Tibullus as
models.

> Cum legerem faciles elegos, Francisce, Marulli,
>   Miratus lepidos cum gravitate iocos,
> Iam quis adhuc, inquam, sani modo pectoris est, qui
>   Vera neget Samii dicta verenda senis?
> Cernimus en culti mentem remeasse Tibulli,
>   Corpore conclusam, culte Marulle, tuo.

[Franciscus, whenever I read Marullo's deft elegies, admiring the
combination of charming jests and weightiness, I say, "who is
there now of sound intellect who would deny that the venerable words of old Pythagoras are true?" Behold! We see the
mind of elegant Tibullus has returned, encased in your body,
elegant Marullo!]

While the *pointe* playfully invokes the Pythagorean concept of trans-
migration of the souls, the poem retains considerable force, especially
in the surprising apostrophe to Marullo and the gemination of the
epithet "cultus." The hyperbole is effective, in part, because it is a
self-conscious exaggeration (and, therefore, has a light irony), though
the tribute to Marullo's art remains forceful: *being* Tibullus, Marullo
"embodies" the model of Renaissance imitative erotic art.

But Secundian love, as is also true for Marullo's poetry, does not
always resemble the gentle eroticism one might associate with Tibullus. Secundus's vigor resides in graphic descriptions of sexual desire
as well as purposeful descents to the level of obscenity. For example,
with a tone of insouciance, he celebrates the affairs of a married
woman and two men (1.10); the sexual encounter can, furthermore,
be repeated *ad libitum*, as the husband has been thoroughly duped:

---

[1] The Catullan terminology is strongest in line 2: "lepidos ... iocos."

Marullus Variusque[1] Septimillae
Donavere toga nova maritum.
Nunc ille ambulat huc et huc togatus,
Et transit fora, porticus, tabernas,
Vicos, balnea, fornices, popinas,
Nec toto decies revisit anno
Relictam dominis domum novellis.
Securi modo saepe luce prima,
Securi modo saepe sole sero,
Securi medio die fruuntur
Marullus Variusque Septimilla.[2]

[Marullus and Varius gave Septimilla's husband a new toga. Now he walks everywhere clad in a toga! He goes through the forums, porticos, taverns, neighborhoods, bathhouses, brothels, and bistros. Nor does he revisit his house, turned over to new masters, ten times in an entire year. Secure at dawn, secure in the evening, secure at midday, Marullus and Varius enjoy Septimilla often.]

With exaggerated rhetorical devices (alliteration, climactic *accumulatio*, and anaphora), Secundus emphasizes the subject of repetition and also, though without a specific source, suggests Catullan invective. The repetition of the first line in the finale, for example, is a common device of Catullus's obscene poems.[3] Similarly, Secundus puts the stamp of a classical style on his obscene tirade on the ugliness of the women of Bourges (*Epigrams* 1.76). He concludes it with an imitation of Tibullus's threats to punish Marathus's promiscuity:

His (i.e., ugly women of Bourges) tamen accumbunt
        iuvenes, dignaeque videntur
Cum quibus extensa proelia nocte gerant.
Illos posse putem rabidae concumbere tigri,
        Inque cruentatas turpiter ire lupas.

(lines 7–10)

---

[1] MS. Rawl. G. 154, fol. 126, "Variusque" is an emendation of a crossed out name (which is now illegible).

[2] Ibid., fol. 127, "fruuntur ... Septimilla" is an emendation of the crossed out "dolabunt ... Septimillam."

[3] See Catullus 16, 36, 52, 57, and 112.

[Nonetheless, the young men go to bed with these women and
the women seem to them to be worthy of the long, nocturnal
battles. I should think that those young men could go to bed
with a fierce tiger or, wickedly, go against bloody wolves.]

In the recasting of Tibullus, Secundus creates an even harsher image
of indiscriminate sex.[1] The comparison of the women to "lupae"
probably is intended to associate them with prostitution, though,
above all, one is left with the intentionally offensive image of bestiali-
ty.[2]

Obscene sex functions not only as a device of the invective epigram, but also as Secundus's defense of poetic license. This can be
seen most clearly in a group of epigrams that revile grammarians. In
Epigrams 1.18, grammarians represent, and are lampooned as, the
source of a restrictive code of poetic decorum. One of Secundus's
longest epigrams, it begins with an extensive invitation to Jerónimo
de Zurita (1512–1580) to visit him at a modest country estate. The
invitation has Vergilian and, above all, Catullan echoes.[3] Zurita is to
bring "quidquid habes facetiarum / Et quidquid salis, atque risionis" (all
the witty stories, jests, and bon mots you have; *Epigrams* 1.18.21–22).
Initially, in fact, the poem seems to be little more than an imitation
of Catullus's humorous dinner invitation to Fabullus (Catullus 13).
While Catullus creates a light tone by inviting the guest to bring all
the food (and, more importantly, wit), Secundus implores Zurita not
to bring a grammarian, as that would spoil the rustic *locus amoenus*.
Specifically, the grammarian must be excluded since he, as an audience, will reject Secundus's poetry. In typical fashion, he concludes
the poem, which began with a charming and refined description of

---

[1] The Tibullan source is 1.9.75–76: "Huic tamen accubuit noster puer: hunc
ego credam / cum trucibus venerem iungere posse feris" (Nonetheless, my boy
lay with him and I think he would be able to have sex with savage beasts).

[2] Moreover, Secundus intended several other epigrams to be equally offensive. For example, he lampoons a lover named Ponticus in *Epigrams* 1.70: "At-
trectans digito muliebria, laeserat ungue / Ponticus: hunc resecat dente: venustus
homo est." The sarcastic "venustus," like the surprising punch-line, is reminiscent of Catullus (see Catullus 22.2).

[3] Line 6 ("qua fagus patulis commata ramis") suggests, at least slightly,
Vergil, *Eclogues* 1.1, and Bosscha associates the image of line 5 ("Si lenis tremula
quies in umbra") with Vergil, *Eclogues* 5.5 ("sive sub incertas Zephyris mo-
tantibus umbras").

bucolic quietude, with a sexual innuendo of an unnamed grammarian, narrated in the style of a Renaissance *facetia*:

> Nam quidam mihi retulit poeta,
> Notae Grammaticum severitatis
> Noctes atque dies dolenter angi,
> Quod nec Grammaticum vocare doctum,
> Nec se Grammaticam vocare doctam
> In libri titulo sui venusti
> Possit, cum generis sit ipse neutri:
> Cui vates meus, ut gravi labore
> Iam tandem miserum senem levaret,
> Secure pater, inquit, eloqueris,
> Si te Grammaticosque masculinos
> Tecum, Grammaticosque femininos,
> Communesque simul, simulque neutros,
> Omnes, Grammaticum pecus vocabis.
>
> (*Epigrams* 1.18.32–45)

[For a certain poet told me that a grammarian of well-known severity was grievously vexed night and day because he was unable to call himself a learned "grammaticus" or a learned "grammatica" in the title of his charming book, as he was, actually, of neither gender. To alleviate the hard efforts of this poor old man, my poet said to him: "You will speak without worry, father, if you will call yourself, and all the masculine grammarians along with you, and all the female grammarians, and all those of both common and neuter gender the 'grammarian herd!' "]

The ending (lines 42–45), with its strident repetitions, finds a suitably invective climax in the appellation "grammarian herd," the circumlocution that avoids the "gender problem" of the emasculated grammarian. While gender has obvious grammatical pertinence, the sexual innuendo discredits, with considerable irony, the implicit literary standard of poetry without sex. The invitation itself—until it turns at line 25 to the attack on grammarians—ingeniously evokes the antique style. Catullan and Vergilian reminiscences, not to mention the fluent hendecasyllabics, make the poem a model of humanist verse, it would seem. Obscenity, which presumably accounts for the poem's unacceptability, emerges only when Secundus claims a distance between his poetry and the rhetorical stricture of decorum. The central idea of distance is, in fact, present both in the initial image of bucolic withdrawal and the concluding invective assault on the grammarian. This curious interplay between imitation of antique style and rejection of the grammarian (presumably a source of philological/imitative poetry) indicates once again that Secundus conforms to a rigid stricture of form (that of classical Roman poetry) but rejects the need to conform to an imposed poetic ideal. In this respect, it is important to note that Secundus often uses Roman sources in his obscene poetry. The sexual invective against the grammarian, for example, may be based on an epigram of Ausonius.[1] What Secundus ultimately does in an epigram such as this one is to ironize conventionality without, I would stress, superseding it.

Epigrams 1.73 mocks the moralistic literary code of the "grammatici" with a similar display of obscenity. The poem opens, in the voice of the poet, with an earnest sounding invocation to the grammarians to speak out, and immediately devolves into a mock scholarly analysis:

> Dicite, Grammatici, cur mascula nomina cunnus,
> Et cur[2] femineum mentula nomen habet?
> Sic ego: sic aliquis senior de gente verenda
> Retulit, attollens longa supercilia:
> Mentula feminei gerit usque negotia sexus;
> Inde genus merito vindicat illa sibi.
> Indefessus agit res qui sine fine virorum,
> Mascula non temere nomina cunnus habet.

["Grammarians, tell us why 'cunt' (cunnus) is a masculine noun and 'prick' (mentula) is a feminine noun?" Thus I spoke. And thus an older member of the reverend race, raising his mighty eyebrows, responded: "The 'prick' does the business of the feminine gender, wherefore its gender is vindicated. The 'cunt', which indefatigably and without end performs the affairs of men, is a masculine noun with good cause."]

---

[1] See also Martial 1.35 for the motif of schoolmasters and obscenity.

[2] MS. Rawl. G. 154, fol. 150, "et cur" is an emendation of the crossed out "cur male."

The sustained mockery of the grammarian ("senior de gente verenda" and "attollens longa supercilia") sets the tone for the ironic "justification," as it were, of obscene diction. Serious words such as "merito" and "non temere," of course, only stress the incongruity of the analysis. The scientific language is humorous but also revealing, as the grammarian is unable, on his own, to express in frank terms the act of making love. He can only use odd euphemistic circumlocutions: "feminei gerit ... negotia sexus" and "agit ... res ... virorum." Nonetheless, the vulgar words "cunnus" and "mentula" can be mentioned unabashedly as they are but the *lemmata* of the scholarly gloss. Furthermore, Secundus heightens the sexual innuendo by implying that the grammarian, though unable to name it, has a vivid image of sex in mind,[1] since he describes intercourse rather extravagantly (though naively), suggesting a kind of insatiability ("usque ... Indefessus ... sine fine").

Epigrams 1.24 and 1.58 defend the erotic poetics of license with specific reference to Secundus's *Basia*. 1.24 is an ironic protestation that two women, inappropriately, have questioned his virility:

> Casta quod enervi cantamus Basia libro,
>   Versibus illudit fusca Lycinna meis;
> Et me languiduli vatem vocat Aelia penis,
>   Quae Venerem in triviis porticibusque locat.
> Scilicet exspectant nostrum quoque noscere penem!
>   Parcite turpiculae, mentula nulla mihi est.
> Nec vobis canto, nec vobis basia figo:
>   Ista legat teneri sponsa rudiș pueri.
> Ista tener sponsus, nondum maturus ad arma,
>   Exercet variis quae Venus alma modis.

[Because I sing of chaste "Kisses" in a languorous book, dark Lycinna mocks my poetry and Aelia calls me the poet of the little limp penis. She sells herself on the streets! Indeed, they expect also to get acquainted with my penis. Stop it, you wicked women! I don't have a penis! I neither sing nor make "Kisses" for you. May the simple bride of the gentle boy read them and the gentle bridegroom, not yet mature for the wars which nurturing Venus exercises in different ways.]

---

[1] See *Basia* 12 (discussed in chapter four) for a similar suggestion that the would-be puritanical audience is actually interested in sexually explicit poems.

As so often in Secundus's epigrams, 1.24 recalls the bawdiness of Catullus and Martial. Catullus, for example, speaks of a "languid penis" in 25.3 ("pene languido senis") and occasionally suggests that, on the basis of his poetry, his virility has been called into question.[1] More importantly, Secundus draws on Martial 3.69, which, especially when read in conjunction with 3.68, is a defense of a sexually crude style. Secundus's contrast of "casta ... basia" and "mentula" evokes Martial's sarcastic praise of a poet named Cosconius for composing poems in "castis verbis" without any "mentula."[2] Obviously, in Martial "mentula" has the transferred sense of obscenity, a meaning which Secundus also exploits. Cosconius's "words should be read by boys and little girls," while Martial asserts that he writes for the debauched or tormented lovers (see lines 5–6). Whereas Marital ironizes the chaste, but boring author, Secundus directs irony at himself with his emphatic, but untenable, insistence that his *Basia* are free of obscenity. Moreover, Secundus associates poetry once again with sex. This is clear in the ironic claim "mentula nulla mihi est" (line 6) and the placement of the kiss-poems in an "*enervi* ... libro" (line 1).[3] And, of course, the conclusion professes a genuine interest in eroticism, though here again literary style is suggested by the phrase "variis ... modis" (line 10).[4]

---

[1] See, for example, Catullus 16.1–4: "Pedicabo ego vos et irrumabo, / Aureli pathice et cinaede Furi, / qui me ex versiculis meis putatis, / quod sunt molliculi, parum pudicum."

[2] See Martial 3.69:

Omnia quod scribis castis epigrammata verbis
    Inque tuis nulla est mentula carminibus,
Admiror, laudo; nihil est te sanctius uno:
    At mea luxuria pagina nulla vacat.
Haec igitur nequam iuvenes facilesque puellae,
    Haec senior, sed quem torquet amica, legat.
At tua, Cosconi, venerandaque sanctaque verba
    A pueris debent virginibusque legi.

[I admire and praise you because you write all your epigrams with chaste words and there is no penis in your poems (i.e., there is no obscenity). Absolutely no one is holier than you. Yet not even a single page of mine is without licentiousness. Therefore, may worthless boys and easy girls read these, and, rather, an old man whose girlfriend torments him. But your venerable and holy words, Cosconius, should be read by boys and maidens.]

[3] Note that there is a pun here as "enervus" could mean "without a penis" or, at least, "unmanly."

[4] Such an association between sex and poetry in the concept of variation

Epigrams 1.58, as indicated by its title, "Ad Grammaticos, cur scribat lascivius" (To the Grammarians, Why He Writes Rather Lasciviously), justifies salacious writing.[1]

> Carmina cur spargam cunctis lasciva libellis,
> Quaeritis? insulsos arceo Grammaticos.
> Fortia magnanimi canerem si Caesaris arma,
> Factave divorum religiosa virum,
> Quot miser exciperemque notas, patererve lituras!
> Quot fierem teneris supplicium pueris!
> At nunc uda mihi dictent quum basia carmen,
> Pruriat et versu mentula multa meo,
> Me legat innuptae iuvenis placiturus amicae,
> Et placitura novo blanda puella viro,
> Et quemcumque iuvat lepidorum de grege vatum
> Otia festivis ludere deliciis.
> Lusibus at laetis procul hinc absistite, saevi[2]
> Grammatici, iniustas et cohibete manus;
> Ne puer ob molles caesus lacrymansque lepores,
> Duram forte meis ossibus optet humum.

[Why do I scatter lascivious poems in all my little books, you ask? I ward off the insipid grammarians! Were I to sing of the doughty arms of the high-spirited emperor, or the religious deeds of saints, how many censures would wretched I receive, or how many corrections endure? To how many tender boys would I become a torment? But, now, since moist kisses dictate my poems and the penis often burns in my verse, let a young man about to please an unwed girlfriend and a sweet girl about to please a young husband read me!—and whoever from the troupe of witty poets likes to play away the leisure time with humorous, erotic poems. Raging grammarians, go far away from these happy trifles and check your unjust hands, lest a

---

also occurs in the *Basia*. See, for example, *Basia* 10, especially lines 18–22.

[1] This poem, which refers to the *Basia* (with links directly to *Basia* 9, 12, and 14), was deleted from the edition of 1541. MS. Rawl. G. 154, fol. 143–44, has the entire poem crossed out.

[2] MS. Rawl. G. 154, fol. 144, line 13 is an emendation of the crossed out "Lusibus at saevi (?) procul hinc abstitite laetis."

schoolboy, beaten and crying on account of my soft, charming poems, implore the earth to lie hard on my bones.]

This is also a highly imitative poem; the diction ("lepidus," "otium," and, of course, "mentula") imbues a Catullan coloration, though other poets are also evoked.[1] The poem's form, a modified *recusatio*, harks back to ancient practices, in particular the poetry of Ovid and, to a degree, Horace. Unlike the ancient *recusatio*, which is a "refusal" to write epic, Secundus's is not merely a vow of allegiance to the lighter (and consequently less significant) art of lyric. Rather, his epigram claims liberty to write as he wishes. Imitating the Horatian "odi profanum vulgus et arceo" (*Odes* 3.1.1), he inveighs against schoolmen: "insulsos arceo Grammaticos" (line 2). But, most importantly, *Epigrams* 1.58 defines Secundus's transgressive poetics with a vivid image: "Pruriat et versu mentula multa meo" (Often the penis burns in my verse; line 8). In a somewhat gentler tone, he claims that his works are intended for those interested in pleasure, be they boys, girls, or poets. Predicting the grammarians' opposition to erotic poetics (line 5),[2] he desires separation from a literary code of decorum and, furthermore, protests the grammarians' compulsion as a type of violence (lines 13–14). The touching image of the concluding couplet stresses the desire for detachment from literary standard. In fact, he has cultivated the graphic style, he says, to preclude incorporation of his poetry in the school curriculum, thus saving his own poetry from becoming a device of oppression. The savage grammarians must stay away from happy literary games ("lusibus").

Secundus also defends love itself (as opposed to poems about love or sex) from social constraints. *Epigrams* 1.52, an address to young men worried, it seems, about pursuing trysts in church, gently (and humorously) elevates love beyond social principles of decorum.

> State cum pulcris iuvenes puellis,
> Iungite et dextras, neque templa, nec vos
> Ara divellat veneranda Divum:

---

[1] As Bosscha noted, line 9 ("Me legat innuptae iuvenis placiturus amicae," etc.) recalls Propertius 1.7.13 ("me legat assidue post haec neglectus amator" [afterwards, may the neglected lover read me constantly]).

[2] It is perhaps ironic that Bosscha, a grammarian of a later age, carps at the poem (specifically, the use of "forte"). See BB, 1:341.

Quin inauratae temerentur arae
Aureo pro basiolo puellae.
Laedit, et magno hic pudor est pudori.[1]

[Young fellows, stay there with the beautiful girls. Embrace and
don't let the churches or the venerable altars of the gods divide
you. Indeed, the gilded altars should be desecrated in order to
get a golden little kiss from the girl. Shame is a violation and a
great shame here.]

Secundus constructed this epigram carefully, with parallelism in the
imperatives ("State . . . Iungite") and the comparison of altars and the
kiss ("inauratae . . . aureo"). He also uses interlocking word order (as
for example in line 1 "pulchris iuvenes puellis") and, as required for
the consummate epigram, saves an elegant and emphatic phrase for
the one-line *pointe* (line 6). Nonetheless, the poem reinforces the
Secundian interpretation of love as a potentially transgressive act of
opposition to cultural restrictions. Indeed, despite the casualness of
the tone and the distancing achieved by the antique setting ("templa"
and "divum"), Secundus claims the right, however artificially formu-
lated, to "desecrate" ("temere") the altars of the church with love.

Taken together, the *Epigrams* illustrate that Secundus's poetics
entails mediation between ideals of stricture and license. Graphic descriptions of sexuality and frequent use of obscenity imitate, in part,
classical style. Because of the classical refinement, some epigrams
could be said to evince a style of "refined crudity." And, indeed, his
latinity deepens the tensions and ironies of his transgressive poetics
since only an elite audience can understand and appreciate the complexity of his imitative obscenity. Moreover, Secundus cultivates the
obscene, albeit humorously, to offend and discredit an audience seeking to impose a moralistic poetics. This ideal of poetic license is, I
think, an important source of the individuality of his poetic voice. Even
at his most vulgar, he conforms to an imitative aesthetic. But, in a basic
shift in the function of obscenity, he uses it to reject conformity to
certain political or moralistic understandings of imitative art.

---

[1] Schoolfield, *Janus Secundus*, 123, draws an interesting parallel between this
poem and Celtis's famous "Ad Sepulum disidaemonem," indicating, however,
Secundus's overriding interest in the erotic sphere. But, as Schoolfield notes,
Secundus did not know Celtis's poetry.

6 *Politics and the Poet of Love*

Bellaque resque tui memorarem Caesaris, et tu
Caesare sub magno cura secunda fores...
Propertius 2.1.25-6 (addressing Maecenas)

[I would celebrate the wars and deeds of your Caesar and you
would be my second subject, after great Caesar...]

Sometime in 1535, Secundus wrote a poetic epistle, addressed to
Diego Hurtado de Mendoza (1503-1575), reaffirming his adherence
to amatory poetics. One of his most elegant poems, *Poetic Epistles* 2.6
locates the poet, to paraphrase lines 11-13, in the shade of a myrtle,
whose crown is buffeted by the vernal Zephyr, where nature com-
miserates with the poet over his lost loves.[1] The opening of the
poem rejects a request from Mendoza for loftier poetry, which in
this context, we can safely assume, meant a Caroline epic:

Didace, quid frustra vatem, levioribus olim
Adsuetum numeris, urges ad grandia verba?
Carminaque integris solide constantia membris?
Qualia, cum magni caneret primordia mundi,
Floridus insonuit grandi Lucretius ore?
Magnos magna decent: rivos ego parvaque quaero
Flumina; nec ventos, sed lenem persequor auram.
(*Poetic Epistles* 2.6.1-7)

---

[1] See *Poetic Epistles* 2.6.11-13: "An me potius myrti iuvet umbra venustae,
/ Quae gracilem vernis Zephyris impulsa coronam / Commiserata meos mecum
suspiret amores?" (Or, rather, may the shade of the charming myrtle give me
pleasure, which, while its graceful crown is buffeted by the vernal Zephyrs,
sighs, commiserating in my loves).

[Diego, why do you vainly urge a poet so long accustomed to lighter metrics to write epic words and poetry thoroughly uniform, in whole verses of hexameter, the kind which florid Lucretius intoned from his grand mouth when he sang of the origins of the great earth? Lofty songs become lofty men. But I seek the streams and little rivers; I pursue not the wind, but the light breeze.]

Though declining to do so in serious compositions, this poem actually uses the "grand words" of hexameter, perhaps as a convenient demonstration that Secundus, despite his professed aversion, was capable of writing in the epic meter. Nonetheless, both the description and the use of the hexameter are somewhat ironic. Hexameter is characterized as the whole or intact verse, as opposed, implicitly, to the lesser (incomplete) pentameter of amatory verse. The hexameter also lends itself to the mock-heroic moment, as we find it in the hyperbolic description of Lucretius's grandiloquence (lines 3–4).

The external circumstances, as far as they can be surmised, give the poem a special place in Secundus's oeuvre. Mendoza was a poet who, among other things, accompanied Charles V on his campaign in Tunisia.[1] Secundus, too, had been expected to join the expedition in order to record its achievements in verse, but illness compelled him to forgo those plans. One might assume, therefore, that Secundus composed this poem after it became clear that he would not be required (or able) to serve as the war's poet. Using Lucretius's memorable passage from the beginning of Book Two,[2] Secundus situates himself in a landscape of peace, from which he can see, in the distance, the difficulties besetting those who tempt the ocean on such military exploits. This, certainly his last, *recusatio* is the only example we have of Secundus distancing himself from what we have reason to believe was an actual commission to write political poetry.

The prominence of the *recusatio* in his oeuvre as well as this retreat from an actual commission raise a question about Secundus's amatory aesthetic. Did he face pressure to write "lofty words for lofty subjects"? Would that explain the intensity of the self-defenses in his love poetry? While one should retain this as a possibility, I

---

[1] For information on Secundus's Spanish acquaintances, see Malkiel, "Juan Segundo."

[2] See Lucretius, *De rerum natura* 2.1–6.

think that, in the absence of more evidence, external pressure probably does not account for the defensiveness of his poetry. Secundus's *recusatio* is a device of self-definition—its prominence is just one aspect of the extensive poetological self-reflection in his oeuvre. Furthermore, any complaints about writing occasional poetry should be taken with a grain of salt. Once, Nicolaus Grudius sent a humorous complaint[1] to Secundus and Marius, protesting the short notice he had been given for composing some adulatory poetry for the funeral procession of Margaret of Austria: "Putant nimirum ignari isti aulici carmina nobis in arboribus nasci, aut cacari"[2] (Undoubtedly, those stupid courtiers think that poems grow on trees for us, or that we shit them). Grudius, however, cheerfully wrote the poem and, apparently pleased with himself, sent it to his brothers for their opinion.

There is, in fact, no need to see amatory poetry in opposition to political life since it certainly had a role, albeit probably a small one, in court entertainment. After all, Gombert, Charles's court composer, set Secundus's erotic "Ode to Love" (*Odes* 10) to music. Moreover, Secundus's contemporary audience, as far as the slight records indicate, were those who walked in his circles at court and at universities. That amatory poetry does not reject political life does *not* mean that it does not reject political poetry. It does, and the distinction between life and poetry is important here. Secundus's aesthetic, which was formed, in part, in the crucible of courtly artistic culture, made the erotic a distinctive form of humanist poetry that eschewed the constraints on poetry concerned with political topics, events, or figures. In Secundus's oeuvre, love poetry exists perpetually, it seems, in opposition to the idea of "public," political literature.

Nonetheless, Secundus did write some political poetry, all of which was consonant with Hapsburg interests. The presence of this political verse does not undermine the integrity of his defense of an amatory aesthetic; it merely establishes an actual contrast, showing that at times Secundus recorded events from political life and, furthermore, did need to praise Charles V in poetry. But given the

---

[1] This letter also gives a brief glimpse into the way political occasional poetry was commissioned. The Hapsburg court provided Grudius with the material for the poem in the form of a French summary of Margaret's life and accomplishments.

[2] Quoted from the transcription provided by Endres, *Joannes Secundus*, 211. This letter is not included in the Burmann-Bosscha edition.

intensity of Secundus's rejection of "serious" or political poetry, it is interesting to read the Hapsburg poems from the perspective of his position as a love poet. To what extent does Secundus inject the amatory style—both its content and its tendency toward levity and irony—into his political poetry?

It is fortuitous that we know Secundus did agree, at least once, to compose a political epic. In fact, a fragment of the inchoate *Bellum Tunetanum* (The Tunisian War) survives,[1] giving, I think, an indication of how he might have attempted the very Caroline heroic epic, which later, in the letter to Mendoza, he refused to write.

> Rursus bella parat Caesar: patientia rursus
> Mansueti iuvenis longo devicta dolore est,
> Et violata gravem pietas erumpit in iram.
> Fervere iam video densis maria omnia remis,
> Telluremque armis, coelum splendescere flamma.
> Quid tantum, Fortuna, paras? cui fata minantur
> Tam dirum excidium? quantove cruore redemtam
> Aeternam, Furiae, pacem conceditis orbi?
>
> (Fragment 2)

[Once again Caesar prepares for war; once again a long-standing grief has overtaken the patience of the gentle youth, and his piety, now that it has been violated, has burst into grave anger. Now, I see all the oceans teeming with dense oars and the land with arms; the heavens flashing with flame. Fortune, what are you readying? What do the fates threaten with such dire destruction? Furies, how much slaughter do you require for eternal peace to be restored to the earth?]

Without any comment on how unusual such a poem would be for him, Secundus sent a copy of these eight lines to his brother Everardus Nicolai. Sadly, he wrote the letter from his sickbed in Madrid while suffering from fever. He laconically refers to a planned poem called the "Historia" and even expressed the wish that he might join in the war. The reason for his militaristic urge, though, is poetic: if he participated in the battles, he would be able to imitate Aeneas's fa-

---

[1] It survives in the sixth prose letter (sent to Nicolaus Everardi) which is printed in BB, 2:279–82.

mous words (spoken as he began to narrate to Dido the fall of Troy in Book Two of the *Aeneid*): "Et quorum pars magna fui"[1] (Of these things I was a great part). Indeed, the fragmentary proemium indicates that, as a strategy for the Caroline epic, Secundus's ear was attuned to Vergil's *Aeneid*. Charles will be celebrated as "pius" ("violata . . . pietas"), cast specifically in a religious struggle against the Muslim Tunisians. Secundus, furthermore, wants to make a correlation between his subject and Augustus, using the typology of Aeneas/Augustus that informs the *Aeneid*. One characteristic which does recall Secundus's usual thematics is the longing for peace over war. But the theme of peace, though only introduced and not elaborated, suggests above all an attempt to tie Charles to Augustus. Like Augustus, Charles will create an empire of the entire world and will impose a *Pax Romana*, here an "aeterna . . . pax" (a pronouncement which, for Secundus in 1535, was probably more disingenuous than wishful).

The parallelism between Charles and Augustus informs Secundus's earliest panegyrics, the two odes from 1530 and 1531. As one would expect, Horace was the model for the language of both odes, even more so, I should add, than earlier commentators have noted. Both are written in Alcaic strophes, the most commonly used metrical scheme in Horace's *Odes*, but also in the distinctive stanzaic form of all the so-called "Roman Odes," the concentrated set of six pro-Augustan poems at the beginning of Book Three (*Odes* 3.1–6). Secundus's *Odes* 1, written to commemorate Charles's coronation in Bologna and printed as early as 1530, was one of his first publications.[2]

---

[1] See BB, 2:280: "Omnes homines cum Caesare et pro Caesare pugnare gestiunt; neque nos, si res ad arma venerit, imbelles aut ignavi arguemur, ut tale quid in Historia mea locum habere possit, quale est illud Aeneae: 'Et quorum pars magna fui' " (All men are eager to fight for, and along with, the emperor; if it comes to battle, may I not be thought weak or craven, so that I can have a line in my "historia" like the one in the *Aeneid*: "Of those things I was a great part").

[2] Since the poem was published during Secundus's lifetime, Dekker, *Janus Secundus*, 132–33, offers an overview of the textual transmission. The only significant change made by the brothers for the edition of 1541 was the emendation of "fatis" in line 20 to "superis." This emendation makes the line conform to the metrics of the Alcaic strophe which does not allow substitution of two shorts for a long.

Adeste, magni progenies patris,
Musae, potenti carmina Caesari
    Cantate, quae fides priorum
        Hactenus haud tetigere vatum.
Quae saxa rursum, quae moveant feras,
Aquasque sistant blanda volubiles,
    Quae mulceant aures canore
        Omnium ubique hominum suavi.
Gaudete cives, plaudite, plaudite:
Gaudete quotquot terra tenet bonos,
    Curasque tristes, atque acerbos
        Pellite pectoribus dolores.
Sumsit sacrato debita vertici
Post tot moras tandem diademata
    Ille optimusque, maximusque,
        Ille vagum domiturus orbem.
Erro? anne vati talia fervido
Sagax futuri Cynthius indicat?
    Quaecumque suggeris, precamur,
        Ut Superis rata sint, Apollo!
Et noscat Ortus, noscat et Occidens
Unum potentem Caesara Carolum,
    Quo mitius, clementiusque
        Nil dederuntve dabuntve secla:
Non si recurrant tempora, quae Iovis
Ferunt parentem, falciferum senem,
    Rexisse, cum Fides, Sororque
        Iusta pio superesset orbi.
Ergo querelas ponite lugubres,
Ergo repostum promite Caecubum:
    Haec, haec dies, haec est choreis,
        Haec rutilis decoranda flammis.

[Be present, Muses, offspring of the great father, sing for mighty Caesar songs that have never touched the strings of the ancient poets; songs that move back rocks, captivate wild animals, beautiful songs that make running water stand still, that soften the breezes with the smooth singing of all men everywhere.

    Citizens, rejoice, applaud, applaud. Rejoice as much as the earth has good things. Chase away any sad cares and bitter grief

from your hearts. After such a long delay he has finally received
the deserved crown on his sacred head, he who is greatest and
best and destined to conquer the wandering globe.

Do I err? Doesn't wise Apollo indicate such things of the
future to the eager poet? We pray, Apollo, that the gods will
bring all your indications to pass. Both the East and the West
know Charles, the only potent emperor, than whom no one
ever was or ever shall be kinder and more gracious, not even if
the age should return that they say was ruled by Jupiter's father, the old man with the scythe, when Faith and her just
sister were still available to a pious world.

Therefore, put aside the mournful complaints and bring out
the cellared Caecuban. This, this is a day for dancing; this day
must be adorned with bright torches.]

The dramatic invocation to the Muses gives the poem a lofty, hymnic quality (which is certainly desired in a celebratory ode), but it
also represents the intense poetic self-consciousness incumbent upon
such a panegyric situation. Asking the Muses to sing is but one indication of how heavily tradition weighs in *Odes* 1. To us it may even
appear ironic that the poet, grasping at originality in lines 3–4, expresses his purported uniqueness with a strong echo of the opening
lines of the "Roman Odes," especially Horace's purpose to sing "carmina non prius / audita" (songs never heard before; *Odes* 3.1.2–3).
The invocation, therefore, reaches the stylistic level of the sublime,
but it also, I think, indicates the need for inspiration as Secundus
moves beyond the pale of his usual style and subject. It is perhaps accidental, but nonetheless noteworthy, that some poets of antiquity
invoke the Muses as they turn, usually momentarily, from lighter
poetry to a political subject. One thinks of the young Vergil of the
erotic *Eclogues* with his invocation to the Theocritean muses at the
beginning of his political *genethliacon* ("Sicelides Musae, paulo maio-
ra canamus" [Sicilian Muses, let me sing somewhat grander songs; *Eclogues* 4.1]). The most telling parallel, though, is Horace himself who
included an extensive invocation to the muses in *Odes* 3.4, the center
of the "Roman Odes." The celebration of Charles's coronation,
moreover, recalls the "Cleopatra-Ode" (*Odes* 1.37), especially with its
invitation to drink cellared Caecuban wine in honor of the peace.[1]

---

[1] Line 30 of Secundus's ode is an answer to Horace's "antehac nefas depro-

Most importantly, lines 22 to 27 evoke Horace's *Odes* 4.2.37–40, a panegyric passage from a *recusatio* in which Horace declines to sing tributes to Augustus:

> quo nihil maius meliusve terris
> fata donavere bonique divi,
> nec dabunt, quamvis redeant in aurum
>   tempora priscum.

[The fates and the blessed gods have given the earth nothing greater or better than him—nor shall they, even if time were to return to the golden past.]

Secundus has once again borrowed Horace's apparently heart-felt appreciation of the *Pax Augustana*, especially Horace's comparison of it to the Golden Age (which is implied in the phrase "aurum ... priscum"). The focus on peace, though a forceful device of humanist pro-imperial panegyric, also moves Secundus into the vicinity of his usual subject of love.

The characterization of Charles in Horatian terms reveals the recurrent attempt by Secundus to apply the ancient concept of deification of the emperor to the homage to Charles. The artificiality and transparency of this device of cultural *imitatio* tone down the effect somewhat, but the praise of Charles as god on earth, based on the model of Augustus, demonstrates the lengths to which Secundus was prepared to go in his panegyrics. Unlike others, this poem does not make a deification of Charles explicit. Nonetheless, he does have a "sacred head" and is described as a force that rules, like a god, over the physical globe of the earth, not just over people (line 16). Most importantly, he bears the honorific "optimus maximus" (line 15), which was used for Roman emperors, but always as a conscious derivation from the cultic title "Jupiter Optimus Maximus."

A distinctive feature of Secundus's ode is that it turns a political moment—a celebration of Charles's coronation—into a poetic one. To be sure, Secundus creates a festive tone (especially with the echoes of the "Cleopatra-Ode") and he certainly pays homage to his Caesar. But an unmistakable strategy of the ode is the elevation of the poet's

---

mere Caecubum / cellis avitis" (until now, it was a sacrilege to bring out the Caecuban from the ancient cellars).

office. The invocation to the Muses asks not only for songs never heard before from the ancient poets, but also for songs that can change the course of nature. One may feel the presence of an unspoken Orpheus in these lines, but they serve primarily to set poetry on an equal level with Caesar. Like the powerful songs, Caesar, it is said, will change the world, restoring it to something even greater than the Golden Age. The parallelism becomes poignant within the context of peace. Songs will soften the ears of men with their tunefulness (line 7), just as the world will experience Charles as the kindest and most merciful emperor (line 23). The parallelism also extends to a suggestion that both poet and Caesar are divine. Secundus uses the Augustan concept of the vatic poet ("vates" or priest-poet), though he adopts a rather light tone when he gives the vatic poet access to the mysteries of Apollo.

Elegies 3.2 (a poem that accompanied the presentation of a medallion portrait of Charles V) offers an earnest-sounding praise of the emperor, especially of his religiosity, power, and sense of justice, but also reflects on the power of art. (See the illustration of the medallion, fig. 4.) Here the "sculptor poeta" (line 5) claims, somewhat light-heartedly, that art cannot do Charles justice—so much is lost because Secundus does not have the hands of a Lysippus (line 15). Nonetheless, the medallion, despite its infelicities, possesses the power, according to Secundus, to define Charles for posterity, even if the pages of history and literature should be silent about him:

> Sic vultus si secla tuos venientia cernent,
>   Et pietas illis et tua nota fides;
> Relligioque et mens observantissima iusti,
>   Nulla licet de te charta loquatur, erit.
>   (*Elegies* 3.2.33–36)

[Thus, if future generations will see your features, their piety, your faith, religion, and deep regard for justice will be noted, even if no writings speak of you.]

Similar panegyric strategies inform *Odes* 6, a commemoration of Charles V's return to the Low Countries in 1531. The ancient concept of imperial deification is suggested by the hymnic quality of the ode, especially its many references to prayer. Moreover "numine cuius" (by whose divine will; line 25) transfers the idea of the emperor-god ushering in a *Pax Augustana* to the sixteenth-century Netherlands. To make the connection between peace under Augustus and Charles even closer, Secundus once again imitates Horace. Lines 25 to 36 recall Horace's *Odes* 4.5.[1] Secundus's "per quem per agros tutus it bos" (because of him the cow goes safely through the fields; line 31) is borrowed directly from Horace's "tutus bos etenim rura perambulat" (then the cow walks safely through the countryside; *Odes* 4.5.17). The theme of poetry is less significant than in *Odes* 1, though it emerges in the finale. Charles's peace will restore the muses, long in exile, to the Netherlands: "[Caesar] Ac exsules terra Sorores / Sideribus revocabit altis" (And Caesar will recall the sisters, exiles from the earth, back from the stars; lines 35–36).

The celebratory Alcaic odes have a measured dignity, achieved perhaps by their copiousness and intricacies, but they also have moments of levity. In that respect, theirs is not entirely distinct from the tone of the amatory odes in Alcaic strophes (*Odes* 10 and 11). Nonetheless, other political poems, especially epigrams and, to a lesser degree, some elegies and funeral poems, illustrate even more clearly Secundus's ability to adapt his casual style to earnest subjects.

Elegies 3.12, for instance, uses the poetic strategies of the panegyric odes. Just like *Odes* 6 which invokes "Belga" (the Low Countries) in its celebration of Charles, *Elegies* 3.12 praises Saragossa, using it as a foil for an encomium to Charles. The elegy celebrates the emperor in no uncertain terms as the modern pendant to Augustus. The finale even reencapsulates the propagandistic myth of the reemergence of a *Pax Augustana* in Charles:

> Rex idem, Caesarque idem, mitissimus idem,
>   Qualis ab Augusti non fuit imperio.
>
>   (*Elegies* 3.12.15–16)

[The same man is king, emperor, and the most benevolent, such as has been missing since the empire of Augustus.]

This elegy, though, has considerably more levity than do the odes. For one thing, Secundus uses a poetic conceit to achieve his Augustan *translatio imperii* in the context of the praise of Saragossa. Saragossa had been named, in Latin, "Caesarea Augusta" after Augustus,

---

[1] The simile comparing the Belgians yearning for Charles's return to birds in a nest awaiting their dilatory mother is said to have been inspired by the simile in Horace, *Odes* 4.5.9–16.

who had founded the city as a settlement for his veterans. The tribute to "Caesarea Augusta" is obviously designed as an artful way of locating the second Caesar Augustus in the original's city. Secundus also makes love a prominent topic in the panegyric. In fact, he apostrophizes Caesar's city as a place of beautiful women, associating Venus with the imperial lineage:[1]

> Te blandis, te molliculis Cytherea puellis
> En beat, Augusto proque nepote colit.
>
> (lines 9–10)

[Look, Venus blesses you with beautiful, charming girls and she devotes herself to you for her Augustan descendant.]

Elegies 3.8, a celebration of the Treaty of Cambrai (1529) between Charles and Francis I of France, naturally was an occasion for Secundus's panegyric strategy of associating the Hapsburg dynasty with peace for its subjects. The tribute to peace, especially the images of agrarian tranquility, remind one of Tibullus's anti-war poetry, especially 1.10.[2] Poetry has a prominent role in the pacified world, as the goddess "Pax" returns with the nine Muses:

> Et vos Pierii turba novena chori:
> Quas inter medius radianti vertice Phoebus
> Increpat argutae fila canora lyrae.[3]
>
> (lines 18–20)

[And you (are among her companions), the choir of the nine Muses, in the midst of whom Phoebus, with radiant head, strikes the tuneful strings of his harmonious lyre.]

Secundus also claims the political elegy for his theme of love. At the end of the "Cambrai-Elegy," he announces the outbreak of a new kind of war—the Ovidian lover will now join battles to replace the political wars:

> Vos qui bella prius, iuvenes, aetate virentes,
> Gessistis cruda sanguinolenta manu,

---

[1] Venus was, of course, the mother of Aeneas.

[2] Tibullus 1.10 also inspired Secundus's poetic address to his friend Charles Catz (*Elegies* 2.11).

[3] Dekker, *Janus Secundus*, 125–27, gives a critical text of *Elegies* 3.8.

> Pro dura galea, roseis ornate corollis
>   Tempora, proque tubis sumite plectra manu.[1]
> Bellaque lascivis nocturna movete puellis,
>   Figite et optato vulnera grata loco.
>
> (lines 39–44)

[Young men, blossoming with youth, you who had before waged bloody wars with rough hands, in the place of the hard helmet, adorn your temples with garlands of rose; in the place of war-trumpets, take up the lyre in your hand. And engage nocturnal wars with sexy girls. Make pleasing wounds in desired places.]

Filling military words with amatory meaning is an important device of his antipolitical aesthetic. Here, the depoliticization of military terminology creates a distinctively frivolous amatory-political poem.[2]

Though certainly a genuine tribute to Charles V as he embarked on the Tunisian expedition of 1535 (just as *Elegies* 3.8 is a genuine encomium to the Peace of Cambrai), *Epigrams* 1.17 not only offers the possibility of an ironic reading, but also indicates very clearly Secundus's efforts to conflate political panegyric and amatory poetics.

> Aeneae sanguis, formosi sanguis Iuli
>   Carolus in regnum venit, Elisa, tuum;
> Vindicet a saevo pius ut tua busta tyranno,
>   Armatas ducens per freta mille rates.
> Illius auspiciis prisco reddentur honori
>   Moenia, Romana quae cecidere manu:
> Ergo age, in Aeneadas odium fatale remitte,
>   Spectatumque veni Caesaris ora Dei.
> Crede mihi; dices, huius si ardore perissem,
>   Causa meae fuerat mortis honesta magis.

[Dido, Charles, of Aeneas's blood and the blood of beautiful Julus (i.e., Ascanius), is on his way to your realm, in order that

---

[1] MS. Rawl. G. 154, fol. 73, "proque tubis sumite plectra manu" is an emendation of the crossed out "Pro lituis sumite sistra manu." The brothers, obviously, objected to the intransitive use of "sumite."

[2] The exclamations of line 2 ("io ... io") also recall in a general sense the exclamations of Catullus's epithalamium (Catullus 61), reinforcing the poem's gaiety and its background tones of love.

he, pious Charles, leading a thousand warships across the sea,
might free your tomb from the rule of a cruel tyrant. Under his
auspices, your walls, which had fallen to a Roman hand, will re-
gain their former prestige. Therefore, come, relinquish that
mortal hatred of Aeneas's descendants; come to see the face of
the divine emperor. Trust me; you will say: "If I had perished
for love of him, the cause of my death would have been more
noble."]

One might argue that the tonal levity renders this poem ridiculous—and
that may well be Secundus's intention. To an excessive degree, Charles
wears the trappings of the heroic *Aeneid*. Pleonastically, he is of the
blood of both Aeneas and Ascanius; like his Trojan forebear, he is
"pius." Secundus also invokes Dido as "Elisa," a designation he has
taken from the *Aeneid*. The artificiality of the Roman *ornatus* hints at
the mock heroic. Indeed, the conceit of Dido falling in love with
Charles—which Secundus saves for the humorous *pointe*—also ironizes
the heroic intonations (and, perhaps, the myth that Hapsburg represents
the greatness of Rome). More importantly, the apostrophe to Dido
exudes an amatory spirit, retaining, most tellingly, the lightness of love
poetry for the celebration of a military campaign.

Many of the *Funeral Poems* pertain to Hapsburg dynastic or courtly affairs. In general, the funeral poem (*funer* or *epicedion*) is a versa-
tile genre in Secundus's hands, with a scope similar to that of his
epigrams. Several poems are tributes to deceased family members and
acquaintances (*Funeral Poems* 1, 12, 14, and 21); some are lightly
erotic epitaphs (*Funeral Poems* 6, 13, 15, 17); and others commemorate literary or pedagogical figures (*Funeral Poems* 7, 8, 10, 11, 23).
But as a single group, those poems on political figures, all with a
connection to the Hapsburg interests, dominate (*Funeral Poems* 2–5,
9, 13, 19, 20, and 24–29).

For example, two *epicedia* commemorate Margaret of Austria,
regent of the Netherlands, who died on 1 December 1530 (*Funeral
Poems* 4 and 5). In *Funeral Poems* 4, Margaret addresses her subjects
with benevolent condescension (ironically portrayed?) for the last
time. Apart from the tribute to dynasty, Secundus's main point is
that the regent was an agent of peace. This accolade was natural for
Margaret as she had negotiated the Peace of Cambrai, but Secundus
asserts, wherever possible, that the Hapsburg empire blesses its subjects with its ability to enforce the peace.

Caesaribus proavis, et Caesare clara nepote,
Margareta Austriaci sata semine Maxmiliani,
Illa ego, quae miti rexi moderamine Belgas,
Et per femineas percusso foedere destras
Discordes populos tranquilla pace beavi,[1]
Hic fato depressa cubo, tellus tenebit
Nescio quid nostro de corpore pulveris atri.
Lustra decem vitae Lachesis vix neverat, et mox
Stamina Parca ferox fatalia rupit, iterque
Ire per obscurum nulli remeabile iussit.
At vos plebeo geniti de sanguine, quando
Ferrea nec nobis didicerunt fata, nec ullis
Parcere nominibus, patientius ite sub umbras.

(*Funeral Poems* 4)

[Distinguished by ancestors who were emperors and a descendant who is the emperor, I am Margaret, born from Maximilian's seed; I have ruled the Netherlands benevolently and through that treaty hammered out by women's hands, I blessed the strife-torn people with tranquil peace. I lie here, humbled by fate; the earth shall retain but the black dust of my body. For my life, Lachesis spun scarcely fifty years and soon the harsh Fate broke the fatal threads and ordered me to go on that dark journey from which no one returns. But you, born from plebeian blood, since the iron fates did not learn to spare me nor any of the high born, go unto death with less resistance.]

Though this poem is an unqualified tribute to Margaret as a part of the Hapsburg dynasty, it is noteworthy that Secundus borrows some of its language from Catullus. Line 10 is based on Catullus 3.11–12. Curiously, the other tribute to Margaret (*Funeral Poems* 5) also recalls a Catullan formulation,[2] all of which suggests a mind focused sharply on amatory poetry.

Secundus composed several humorous funeral poems, some of which concerned figures of the Hapsburg court. Of the two poems written upon the death of Mercurino Arborio di Gattinara (died 5

---

[1] MS. Rawl. G. 154, fol. 101, line 5 is an emendation of the crossed out "tranquilla populos et longa pace beavi."

[2] This line recalls Catullus 3.11–12. *Funeral Poems* 5 evokes Catullus 5.6.

June 1530), who had been chancellor to Charles V, *Funeral Poems* 2 is somewhat whimsical, making a pun on Gattinara's first name in order to associate him as well as Charles V with the gods:[1]

> Mercurius moritur. Quid? Maia natus? an ille,
>   Dignus qui Maia, qui Iove partus erat?
> Quem sibi vult socium terrenus Iupiter olim,
>   Sive paret pacem, seu grave Martis opus?
>
> (lines 1–4)

[Mercury has died. What? The son of Maia? Or was it he, worthy to be born to Maia and Jove, whom the earthly Jupiter used to have as a companion, if he prepared for peace or the heavy work of war?]

A broadly humorous tone emerges in a poem on the death of a certain Heduus (a name that would designate a boy from Autun) who was a cupbearer at the court of Charles V. The reflection on his death, with its comparison to Ganymede, suggests that the epitaph was designed not to express bereavement but as a kind of erotic joke for the court.

> Marmorea iuvenem facie croceoque capillo
>   Miscentem nostro pocula casta Iovi,
> Iupiter, aetherias cur, invide, tollis in[2] arces?
>   Quod puer Iliacus, non erit iste tibi.
> Ulta tuum melius numquam Saturnia crimen;
>   Formosum thalamis inferet ipsa suis.
>
> (*Funeral Poems* 13)

[Why, envious Jupiter, did you raise to the heavenly citadel that boy with the marble features and the golden locks, who mixed pure cups of wine for our Jove? He will not be what the Trojan boy was to you! Never has Juno better avenged your sin. She will carry that beautiful boy off to her marriage bed.]

---

[1] The other tribute to Gattinara is *Funeral Poems* 3, which is a good example of the epigrammatic style Secundus often uses in his epitaphs.

[2] I have restored the only manuscript reading here. Burmann-Bosscha print "ad arces" (BB, 2:124).

Political poetry could also be critical, though only of Charles's enemies.[1] Three poems inveigh against Francis I after his breech, in 1536, of the Treaty of Cambrai: two are lampooning epigrams (*Epigrams* 1.25 and 1.26) and one is a mocking farewell to the dauphin, François de Valois, who died on 10 August 1536 (*Funeral Poems* 25). *Epigrams* 1.25, the sharpest of the poems against Francis, makes a triple pun on the word "Gallus," which Secundus uses as an appellation for Francis I: it means Gaul (or Frenchman), cock, and a castrated priest of Cybele, the ancient earth-mother goddess. For the innuendo, Secundus draws upon an epigram by Martial (9.68) and, more importantly, Lucretius's famous description of the "Galli" or priests of Cybele (*De rerum natura* 2.600–660) as well as Catullus's Attis poem (Catullus 63), a work in the extremely rare galliambic meter that narrates Attis's self-castration on the island of the great mother.

> Armigerumne Iovis, volucris cristata, lacessis?
> Tamne cito exciderunt vincula Ibera tibi?
> Quid petis Italiam tam longo, Galle, volatu?
> . Innumeros Gallos illa recondit humus.
> Quod si longinquas cura est tibi visere sedes,
> Idaei montis culmina celsa petas;
> Turritamque colas matrem, et cava tympana palmis
> Concute, et horrisono cornua rauca sono;
> Correptusque furore, hosti quae tela parabas,
> Inguinis haec facias caede cruenta tui:
> Talia namque decent Gallum, non arma movere,
> Et terram bellis concutere et maria.[2]
>   (*Epigrams* 1.25)

[Oh cock with the fancy headdress, are you challenging Jupiter's armbearing eagle? Have you so quickly forgotten those Iberian chains?[3] Cock, why do you seek Italy in such a long flight? That land already has plenty of cocks (or: castrated priests). But if you want to visit far-off places, go to the lofty summits of Mt Ida. Wor-

---

[1] There is one other invective against a ruler: *Epigrams* 1.48, which seems to be a stylistic exercise, inveighs against Nero's cruelty.

[2] This poem did not appear in the edition of 1541. MS. Rawl. G. 154, fol. 132–34, has the entire poem crossed out.

[3] This is a reference to Francis's imprisonment after he had been captured by Charles in 1525.

ship the mother with the turreted crown and beat the hollow tympana with your hands and the raucous horns with their frightful din. Infuriated, bloody those weapons you prepare for your enemy with the gore of your own genitals. For, indeed, that befits a "Gallus" (a priest of Cybele); wielding arms and striking land and sea with wars do not!]

Secundus not only threatens the French cock ("Gallus") with the Hapsburg eagle[1] but also discredits Francis as an effeminate eunuch. It is telling that Secundus, as an amatory poet opposed to epic, makes the potentially heroic image of war into a—for Secundus—humorous idea of sexual self-mutilation. The sexual mutilation, above all, is derived from Catullus 63, representing once again Secundus's attempt to cast the political epigram in a Catullan style.

There is also a set of invectives against Henry VIII, attacking both his divorce from Catherine of Aragon and the execution of Thomas More. As Catherine was part of the Hapsburg dynastic policy,[2] Secundus was obviously opposed to Henry's action. Strangely, as an answer to a poem by Francesco Molza (1489–1544),[3] Secundus also wrote a *heroide*, in which Henry VIII offers an eloquent explanation of his rejection of Catherine. The poem remains very puzzling, despite the unpersuasive effort by Burmann and Bosscha to argue that Henry VIII's justification of the dissolution falls flat.[4] Secundus also wrote an epitaph for Catherine which, though respectful of her dire situation, is principally a political lampoon against Henry:

> Illa ego, quae poteram regi placuisse marito,
>   Et forma, et castis moribus et genere,
> Postquam me thalamis exclusit adultera pactis,
>   Emorior, solo funere grata viro.[5]
>
> (*Funeral Poems* 29)

---

[1] That is also the sense of *Epigrams* 1.26.

[2] The dynastic policy became the subject of an anonymous epigram: "Bella gerant alii, tu felix Austria nube; / Nam quae Mars aliis dat tibi dona Venus" (Let others wage wars, Austria you are blessed by marriage; for the gifts Mars gives to others, Venus gives to you).

[3] Molza's poem was printed by Burmann-Bosscha as *Sylvae* 9; Secundus's poem, written in the voice of Henry VIII, is *Sylvae* 10.

[4] Obviously, Secundus himself did not publish the answer of Henry, and it is impossible to know if he would have, or if he would have altered it.

[5] MS. Rawl. G. 154, fol. 121, has the entire poem crossed out.

[I am she who was able to please her royal husband with beauty, character, and lineage. But after the adulteress drove me out of the legal wedding bed, I perish, pleasing to my husband with my funeral alone.]

Anti-Henry sentiments are strongest in the three commemorations of Thomas More, written after his execution on 6 July 1535. Two are brief poems (*Funeral Poems* 27 and 28) that threaten Henry VIII with punishment in the afterlife. *Funeral Poems* 26, one of Secundus's longer poems, is a rambling lamentation of More's execution.[1] Tributes to More's probity are numerous, including a strong hint that he will be canonized (lines 158–60); there is also a long address to Margaret, More's learned and devoted daughter (lines 92–112). Much of the poem, however, is a visceral attack on Henry as a godless tyrant, a distinctive feature of which is Secundus's growing worry over the fragmentation of the church. For example, in lines 62–70, Henry is damned most emphatically for his rejection of papal authority. The Hapsburg concern for unity in Christendom informs another of Secundus's late poems, a prayer to God asking for deliverance from the tumults of the antibaptists—a certain reference to the debacle in Münster in 1534–1535 (*Odes* 12).

At the end of his residence in Spain, Secundus was, finally, prepared to write political epic, though circumstances thwarted the project. Until then and even afterward, he restricted his political efforts to the genres he had mastered, especially the ode, elegy, epigram, and funeral poem. His glorification of Charles and the idea of Hapsburg *imperium* as a reincarnation of Augustus comes across, in retrospect, as a predictably humanist strategy. The paradigm of *imitatio*, to a degree, lessens the strain of the hyperbolic panegyric: deification of the emperor, after all, is just an ancient device, in this case one drawn from the celebratory odes of Horace and scattered passages in Vergil. Secundus, though, relies on the ancient poets of small forms (the lyricist, elegist, and epigrammatist) who, despite their overriding interest in amatory and philosophical poetry, did compose political poems.

---

[1] For an edition and French translation of the poems on Thomas More, see Blanchard, "Jean Second et ses poèmes sur l'exécution de Thomas More." Blanchard also printed and translated two poems by Nicolaus Grudius on More's execution; see idem, "Poèmes du XVIe siècle à la mémoire de Thomas More et de Jean Fisher."

Horace, thus, became an inspiration, and his focus on the peace of
the empire—a thought one would not be inclined to associate with
Charles V—provided Secundus with a subject for his imperial panegyric. Horace's tributes to the *Pax Augustana*, when imitated for Caroline encomium, also offered a promising transition from the political
to the amatory, as love is depicted as the prime reward of peace.
Beyond these characteristics, it is important to note that Secundus
repeatedly injects the levity of his nugatory poetics into political
poetry. Wars of soldiers became wars of lovers; courtly celebration
is a time for drink and dance; a modern emperor is cast as a suitable
lover for the ancient queen Dido. To be sure, there is not a trace of
reluctance to endorse Charles to the stars, though there remains the
frequent, albeit inconsistent, attempt to conform Caroline poetry to
the trifling aesthetics of love.

7 *A Concluding Note*

His gifts of genius aside, Secundus was most fortunate to have been born into his circumstances of family and society. We have solid evidence that at least three of his older brothers and sisters aspired to be artists or writers. We also know that wherever he went, he moved in the highest levels of society and in a community of, among other things, artists and professionals who, like so many of the humanistically minded, devoted their leisure to letters. And, of course, Mechlin, Brussels, and the itinerant court of Charles V in Spain were extraordinarily receptive to humanist literature. As we have seen, much of Secundus's poetry is written to or for those at court with their own literary and artistic aspirations.

Of more general significance to his development was the high status of Latin as well as the existence of a well-defined erotic tradition in the poetry of Italian humanists. He was born to a moment in literary history when Italian Latin lyric not only had achieved, perhaps, its artistic apex but also had become fashionable, and widely accepted, on the literary scene of northern Europe. As indicated in several foregoing discussions, one cannot read Secundus without hearing the resonance of such poets as Crinitus, Marullo, Sannazaro, and Pontano. In fact, as is apparent in his repeated acknowledgments, Secundus openly styles himself a follower of these Italian erotic poets. In *Elegies* 3.7, he narrates a dream, based on Ovid, *Amores* 3.1, in which the allegorical figure "Elegy" speaks to him. Representing above all amatory elegy, "Elegy" appears as an Italian girl, with an Italian style of dress. (See *Elegies* 3.7, lines 17ff., for the description of the "new adornment" of Italian poetry.) Pontano, for example, is an innovator of erotic poetry, according to Secundus's "Elegy":

> Pontanus, cuius laudibus aura sonat,
> Pontanus, puerum docui quem prima sonare
> Alitis Idalii vincula, tela, faces. (*Elegies* 3.7.28–30)

[Pontano, for whom the breeze sounds with praises, Pontano, whom I first taught in his youth to sing of the chains, weapons, and torches of the winged Idalian.]

Secundus, in turn, developed his poetic idiom in part by studying the Italian pupils of "Elegy." More importantly, the precedent of the Italian humanists—especially the Strozzi, Marullo, and Pontano, all of whom wrote daringly about sexual desire—legitimated erotic licentiousness, at least to a degree.

While it is appropriate to see him as a northern European extension of the Italian love poets—indeed, it was certainly fitting that even in the sixteenth century he was anthologized with such a writer as Marullo[1]—Secundus articulated a distinctive poetic voice. His distinctiveness lies not only in the brilliance of his phraseology, or the vividness of his portrayals of sexual desire, or the blending of life and art in his descriptions of experience, but also in his reflections on the meaning and sociopolitical location of his nugatory poetics; his voice epitomizes and defines the paradox of the transgressive conventionality of his amatory poetics. His poetological reflections, moreover, defend erotic amatory poetry without taking recourse for legitimacy to the "meaningfulness" of allegorical or philosophical forms of love poetry, especially the strong traditions of Petrarchism and neo-Platonic amatory poetry. Instead, he flouts, on occasion, the very idea of legitimacy, consciously transgressing mores while remaining within the borders of the classical and Italian erotic landscape.

Secundus repeatedly stylizes an ideal of life as the experience and pursuit of art. *Elegies* 3.18 records what must strike us today as an unusual "orgy" ("He mixed the gifts of Bacchus with Roman Phoebus"[2]), an evening of wine and poetry reading devoted to Latin works by German authors. (Eobanus Hessus, Georg Logau, and Georg Sabinus are mentioned.) At the end of the poem, he invokes the Muses to express gratitude to a certain Joannes Ottinger (an otherwise unknown German poet) for the introduction to German humanist poetry; like an experience of love, it seems, recollection of that

---

[1] This was the work of Ludovicus Martellus in his edition of *Poetae tres elegantissimi* of 1582. The third poet was Hieronymus Angerianus (c. 1490–1535), another Italian practitioner of the erotic, whose works, however, tend to be flat and unoriginal. He is remembered principally for his coinage of the generic designation "erotopaegnion."

[2] *Elegies* 3.18.23: "Miscuit et Latio Lenaei munera Phoebo."

day will never fade.[1] Poetological reflection is a constant element in
Secundus's poetry, which, like the best of Renaissance lyric, arises as a
conscious struggle between acceptance of convention and the urge to
achieve something different. Secundus, at times, attempts to define
poetry as an artistic discourse raised above (or lowered beneath) the level
of political ideology, while at other times he uses poetry as a medium
for political panegyric, such as the glorification of the Hapsburg empire
as the equivalent of the Augustan *imperium*. In the larger body of his
poetry, however, he repeatedly valorizes artistic experience—the life of
imagination, the power of beauty, the writing of love—over the heavy
(and grounding) momentousness of political history or panegyric.

Nonetheless, politics figures prominently as a negative force in his
love poetry. It is the world of law, convention, order, and serious-
ness—characteristics which are the opposite of his poetic ideals. He
may have been caught in the middle of the contrary poles of an
artistic and a political-bureaucratic life. But such a notion of him
would be entirely speculative, as the evidence for determining his
outlook in life is scanty. Perhaps the compromises of his brothers
who, like so many humanists, kept literary interests alive while pursuing political careers, were unsettling. To its credit, though, the
Caroline court did accommodate such literary interests. Moreover,
Secundus would have found it exceedingly difficult to achieve or
maintain social status and independence on the strength of his writing alone. (Apart from the political life, his only other options as a
humanist would have been academic or ecclesiastical careers.) In his
devotion to art, he was not a Horace. While Horace, according to
Suetonius, repeatedly refused Augustus's attempts to appoint him secretary, Secundus was all too eager for such an office under Charles V.
But, whether or not this tension existed in his life—and we have
every reason to assume that he accepted his career in the Hapsburg
bureaucracy without reluctance—it remains a strong force in his
poetry. Consequently, the apolitical ideal of his amatory world is
highly political. Writing love, he reflects in sensitive and evocative
ways on the connection between art and cultural, social, and political
expectations.

---

[1] See *Elegies* 3.18.33-34: "Quorum me semper memorem fore dicite Musae,
/ Sive prememus humum, sive prememur humo" (Muses, tell him that I shall
always recall all these poets, whether I shall press the earth or the earth shall
press me).

Select Bibliography

Please note that the most complete bibliography of works by and about Secundus is that of Dekker, *Janus Secundus,* 274–96. My list is confined to important editions and studies as well as a few additional works I consulted.

Editions of Works by Janus Secundus

Bodleian Manuscript Rawl. G. 154. Manuscript begins: "Hoc ordine edenda Io. Secundi poëmatia." [This is the manuscript that was used as the printer's copy for the edition of 1541. I have used a microfilm of it.]

Ioannis Secundi Hagiensis Basia. Et alia quaedam. Edited by Michael Nerius. Lugduni: Apud Seb. Gryphium, 1539. [This is the first edition of the *Basia.*]

Ioannis Secundi Hagiensis Opera: nunc primum in lucem edita. Edited by Nicolaus Grudius and Hadrianus Marius. Traiecti Batavorum: Hermannus Borcolous, 1541. [The first edition of the collected works; a facsimile reprint of this is available from Nieuwkoop: de Graaf, 1969.]

Poetae tres elegantissimi, emendati, et aucti, Michaël Marullus. Hieronymus Angerianus. Ioannes Secundus. Edited by Ludovicus Martellus. Parisiis: Apud Dionysium Duvallium, 1582. [First edition to anthologize Secundus with Italian eroticists. Text of Secundus's poems is based on a 1561 Paris edition done by Gulielmus Cripius.]

Poetmata et effigies trium fratrum Belgarum. Nicolai Grudii Nic: Eq. etc. Hadriani Marii Nic: Eq. etc. Ioannis Secundi Nic. Edited by Bonaventura Vulcanius. Lugduni Batavorum: apud Elzivirium, 1612. [An anthology of poetry by the three brothers.]

Delitiae c. poetarum Belgicorum. Edited by Janus Gruterus. 4 vols.

Francofurti: Typis Nicolai Hoffmanni, sumptibus Iacobi Fischeri, 1614. [This is an important anthology, compiled by Gruterus who was a philologist and poet as well as the last librarian of the Palatine Library in Heidelberg.]

Ioannis Secundi Hagiensis, Poetae elegantissimi, Opera quae reperiri potuerunt omnia. Edited by Petrus Scriverius. Leiden: Jacobus Marcus, 1619. [First critical edition of Secundus.]

Iohannis Secundi Opera. Edited by Petrus Scriverius. Leiden: Franciscus Hegerus, 1631. [This is the corrected edition, for which Scriverius used the Bodleian manuscript.]

Ioannis Nicolaii Secundi Hagani Opera omnia. Edited by Petrus Burmannus Secundus and Petrus Bosscha. 2 vols. Leiden: Luchtmans, 1821. [This remains the standard edition, though Alfred Dekker has announced the preparation of a much-needed new edition.]

Basia. Edited by Georg Ellinger. Berlin: Weidmann, 1899. [A critical edition of the *Basia*.]

The Love Poems of Johannes Secundus. Translated by F. A. Wright. London: Routledge, 1930. [The renderings in English are very loose, though some of the phrases are admirable.]

Les baisers et l'épithalame suivis des odes et des élégies. Edited and translated by Maurice Rat. Paris: Garnier, 1938. [This is a large selection of poems with accurate prose translations in French.]

Küsse. Translated by Felix M. Wiesner. Zürich: Waage, 1958. [Example of a fine press edition that stresses Secundus's eroticism.]

An Anthology of Neo-Latin Poetry. Edited and translated by Fred J. Nichols. New Haven: Yale University Press, 1979. Pp. 486–523. [Contains text and translation of *Epigrams* 1.58, *Basia* 1–19 and *Sylvae* 8 (the erotic epithalamium).]

Other Works Cited

Blanchard, André. "Jean Second et ses poèmes sur l'exécution de Thomas More." *Moreana* 9/36 (1972): 1–32.

———. "Poèmes du XVIe siècle à la mémoire de Thomas More et de Jean Fisher." *Moreana* 11/41 (1974): 93–99.

Catullus, Gaius Valerius. *Carmina.* Edited by R. A. B. Mynors. Oxford: Clarendon Press, 1972.

Crane, Dougall. *Johannes Secundus.* Leipzig: Tauchnitz, 1931.

Dekker, Alfred M. M. *Janus Secundus (1511–1536): De tekstoverlever-*

ing van het tijdens zijn leven gepubliceerde werk. Nieuwkoop: de Graaf, 1986.

Ellinger, Georg. *Geschichte der neulateinischen Literatur Deutschlands im sechszehnten Jahrhundert.* 3 vols. Berlin: De Gruyter, 1933.

——. "Goethe und Johannes Secundus." *Goethe-Jahrbuch* 13 (1892): 199–210.

Endres, Clifford and Barbara K. Gold. "Joannes Secundus and His Roman Models." *Renaissance Quarterly* 35 (1982): 282–86.

Endres, Clifford. *Joannes Secundus: The Latin Love Elegy in the Renaissance.* Hamden, Conn.: Archon, 1981.

Erasmus, Desiderius. *Dialogus Ciceronianus.* Edited by Pierre Mesnard. In *Opera omnia,* vol. 1.2:581–710. Amsterdam: North-Holland Publishing Company, 1971.

——. *Opus epistolarum.* Edited by P. S. Allen and H. M. Allen. 12 vols. Oxford: Clarendon Press, 1906–58.

Greek Anthology. Edited and translated by W. R. Patton. 5 vols. London: Heinemann, 1953.

Guépin, J. P. *De Kunst van Janus Secundus: De 'Kussen' en andere Gedichten.* Amsterdam: Bert Bakker, 1991.

Horatius Flaccus, Quintus. *Opera.* Edited by Edward Wickham and H. W. Garrod. Oxford: Clarendon Press, 1967.

Joos, German. "Eenige grieksch-latijnsche en italiaansch-renaissance invloeden op de *Basia* van Janus Secundus." *Revue belge de philologie et d'histoire* 20 (1941): 5–14.

Kidwell, Carol. *Marullus: Soldier Poet of the Renaissance.* London: Duckworth, 1989.

Lucretius Caro, Titus. *De rerum natura.* Edited by Joseph Martin. Leipzig: Teubner, 1969.

Malkiel, María Rosa Lida de. "Juan Segundo y la biografía de varios autores peninsulares de siglo XVI." In *Miscelânea de estudos em honra do Prof. Hernâni Cidade,* 134–67. Lisboa: Imprensa de Coimbra, 1957.

Martial, *Epigrammaton Libri.* Edited by W. Heraeus and Iacobus Borovskij. Leipzig: Teubner, 1976.

Martyn, John R. C. "Ioannes Secundus: Orpheus and Eurydice." *Humanistica Lovaniensia* 35 (1986): 60–75.

——. "The Relationship between Lúcio Ângelo André de Resende and Iohannes Secundus." *Humanistica Lovaniensia* 37 (1988): 244–54.

Marullus, Michael. *Carmina*. Edited by Alessandro Perosa. Zurich: Artemis, 1951.

Molhuysen, P. C. "Julia." *Handelingen en mededeelingen van de matt- schappij der nederlandsche letterkunde* (1910/11): 107–9.

Nichols, Fred J. "The Renewal of Latin Poetry in the Renaissance: Rhetoric and Experience." In *Actes du VIe Congrès de l'Association Internationale de Littérature Comparée*. Edited by Michel Cadot et al., 89–98. Stuttgart: Bieber, 1975.

Ovidius Naso, Publius. *Amores. Medicamina faciei femineae. Ars amatoria. Remedia amoris*. Edited by E. J. Kenney. Oxford: Clarendon Press, 1961.

———. *Metamorphoses*. Edited by William S. Anderson. Leipzig: Teubner, 1977.

Oxford Latin Dictionary. Oxford: Clarendon Press, 1982.

Perella, Nicolas James. *The Kiss Sacred and Profane*. Berkeley and Los Angeles: University of California Press, 1969.

Propertius, Sextus. *Carmina*. Edited by E. A. Barber. Oxford: Clarendon Press, 1960.

Raa, C. M. G. ten. "Everaerts, Nicolaas." *Nationaal Biografisch Woordenboek*, 7:214–31. Brussel: Paleis der Academiën, 1977.

———. "Nicolai, Elisabeth." *Nationaal Biografisch Woordenboek*, 7:652–56.

———. "Nicolai, Everaert." *Nationaal Biografisch Woordenboek*, 7:656–62.

Ronsard, Pierre de. *Oeuvres complètes*. Edited by Paul Laumonier. 8 vols. Paris: Librairie Alphonse Lemerre, 1914–19.

Rupprich, Hans. *Der Briefwechsel des Konrad Celtis*. Munich: Beck, 1934.

Schoolfield, George C. *Janus Secundus*. Boston: Twayne, 1980.

Schroeter, Adalbert. *Beiträge zur Geschichte der neulateinischen Poesie Deutschlands und Hollands*. Berlin: Mayer and Müller, 1909.

Spitzer, Leo. "The Problem of Latin Renaissance Poetry." In *Romanische Literaturstudien 1936–1956*, 921–44. Tübingen: Niemeyer, 1959.

Stallybrass, Peter and Allon White. *The Politics and Poetics of Transgression*. London: Methuen, 1986.

Tibullus, Albus, et al. *Carminum libri tres*. Edited by John Postgate. Oxford: Clarendon Press, 1968.

Tracy, James D. "Everaerts, Nicolaas." In *Contemporaries of Erasmus*.

Edited by Peter G. Bietenholz, 1:446–47. Toronto: University of Toronto Press, 1985.

Trunz, Erich. "Der deutsche Späthumanismus um 1600 als Ständekultur." In *Deutsche Barockforschung.* Edited by Richard Alewyn, 147–81. Cologne and Berlin: Kiepenheuer and Witsch, 1966.

Tuynman, P. "De handschriften en overige bronnen voor de teksten van Secundus." In Guépin, *De Kunst van Janus Secundus,* 201–67.

Van Leijenhorst, C. G. "Nicolaus Grudius." In *Contemporaries of Erasmus,* 2:139–40.

Van Tieghem, Paul. *La littérature Latine de la Renaissance.* 1944; repr. Geneva: Slatkine Reprints, 1966.

Vergilius Maro, Publius. *Opera.* Edited by R. A. B. Mynors. Oxford: Clarendon Press, 1976.

Vocht, Henry de. *John Dantiscus and His Netherlandish Friends As Revealed by Their Correspondences, 1522–1546.* Louvain: Vandermeulen, 1961.